Woman in Dunes... A memory, a mirage, an infatuation that I had in my imaginative youth.

One does not dance to reach a destination.

- Tim Gallo.

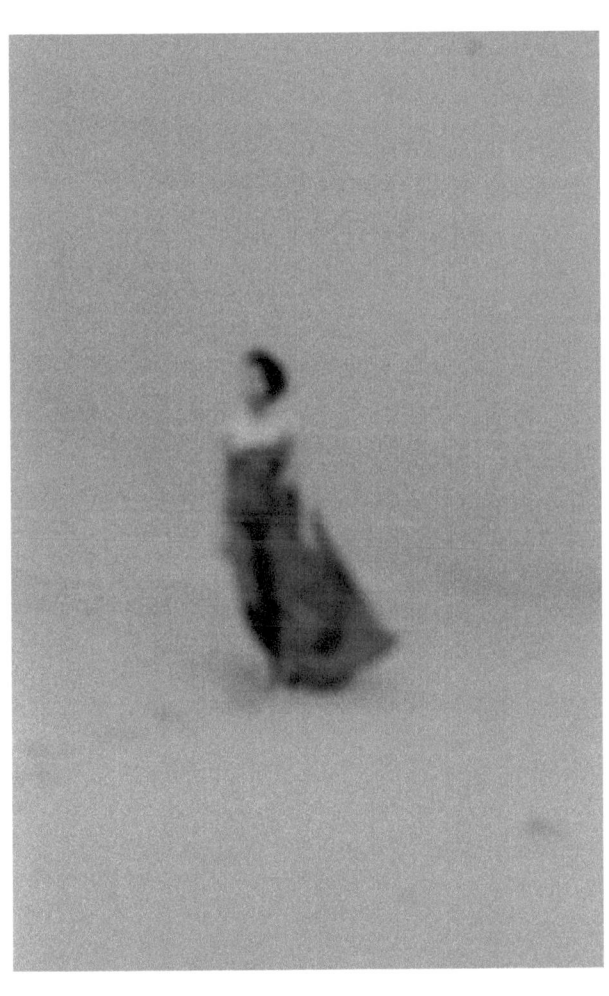

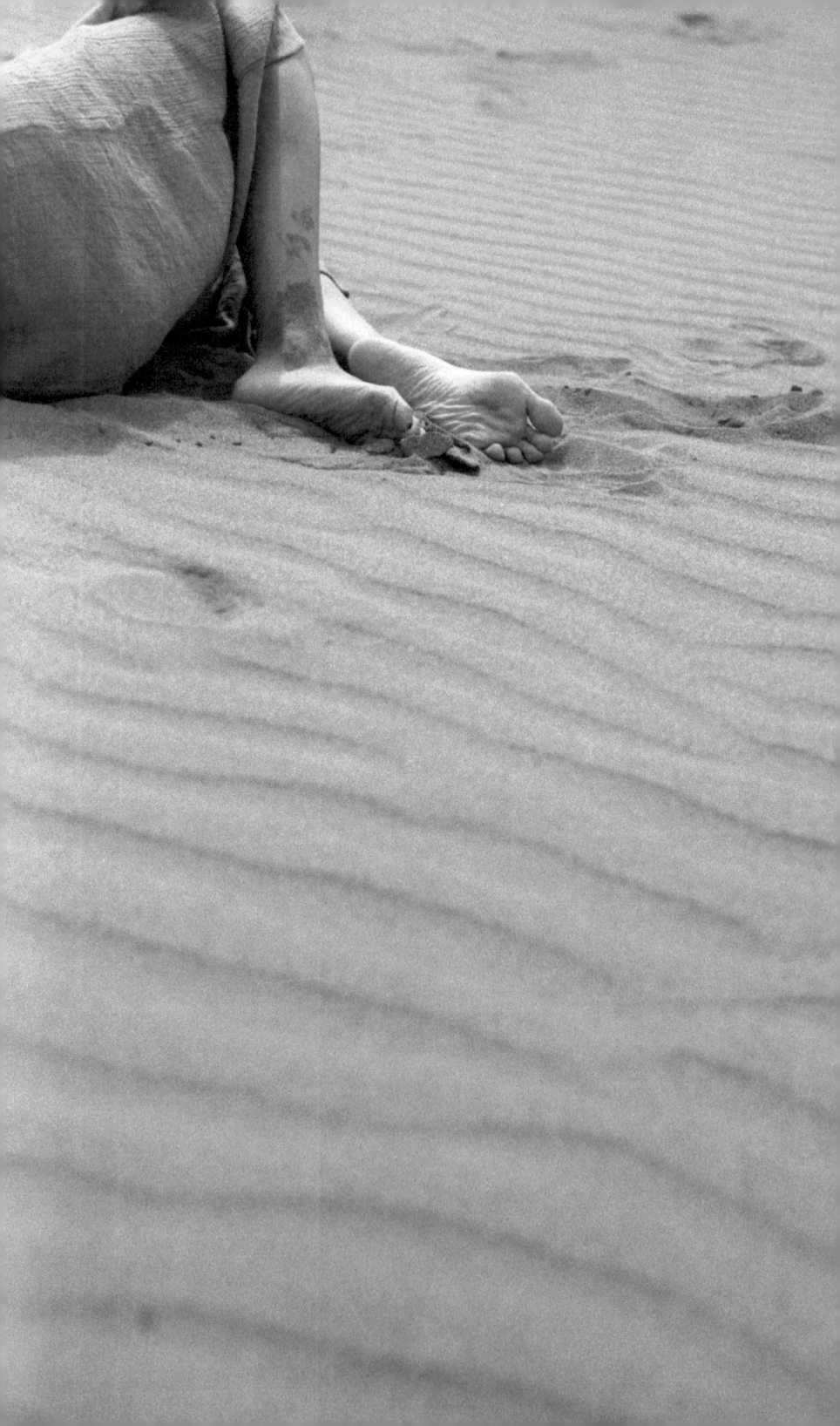

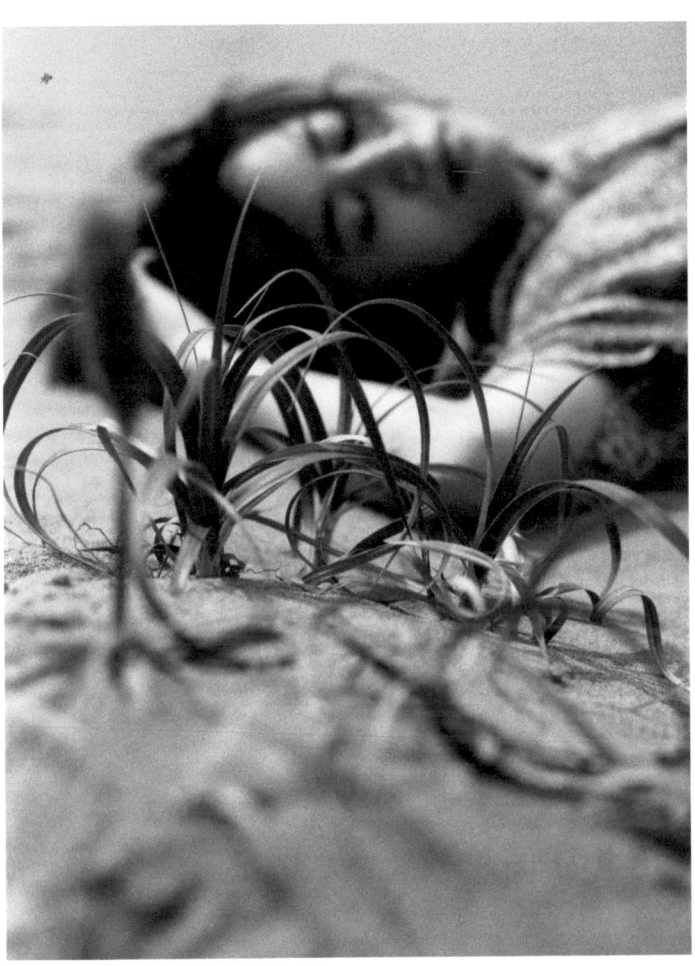

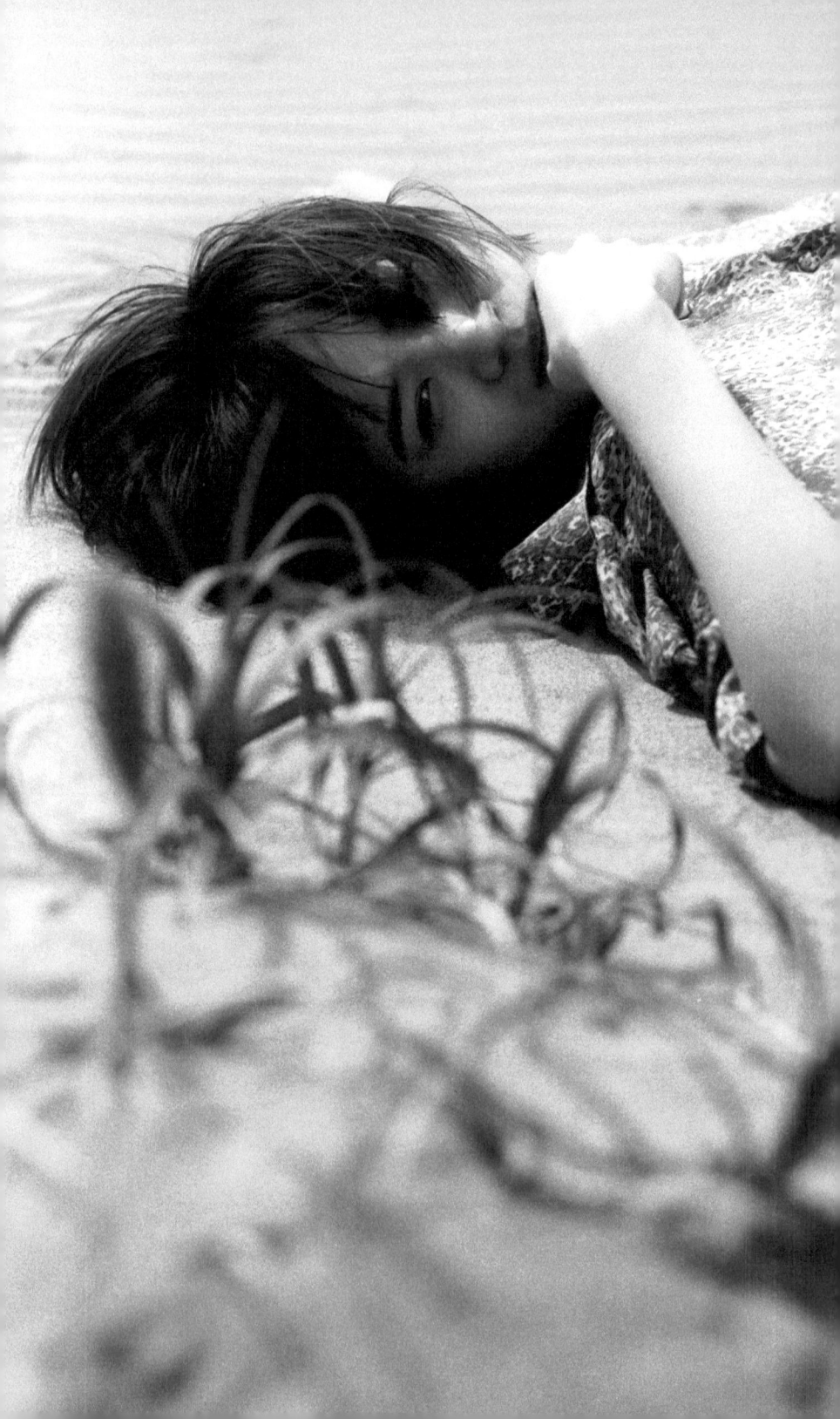

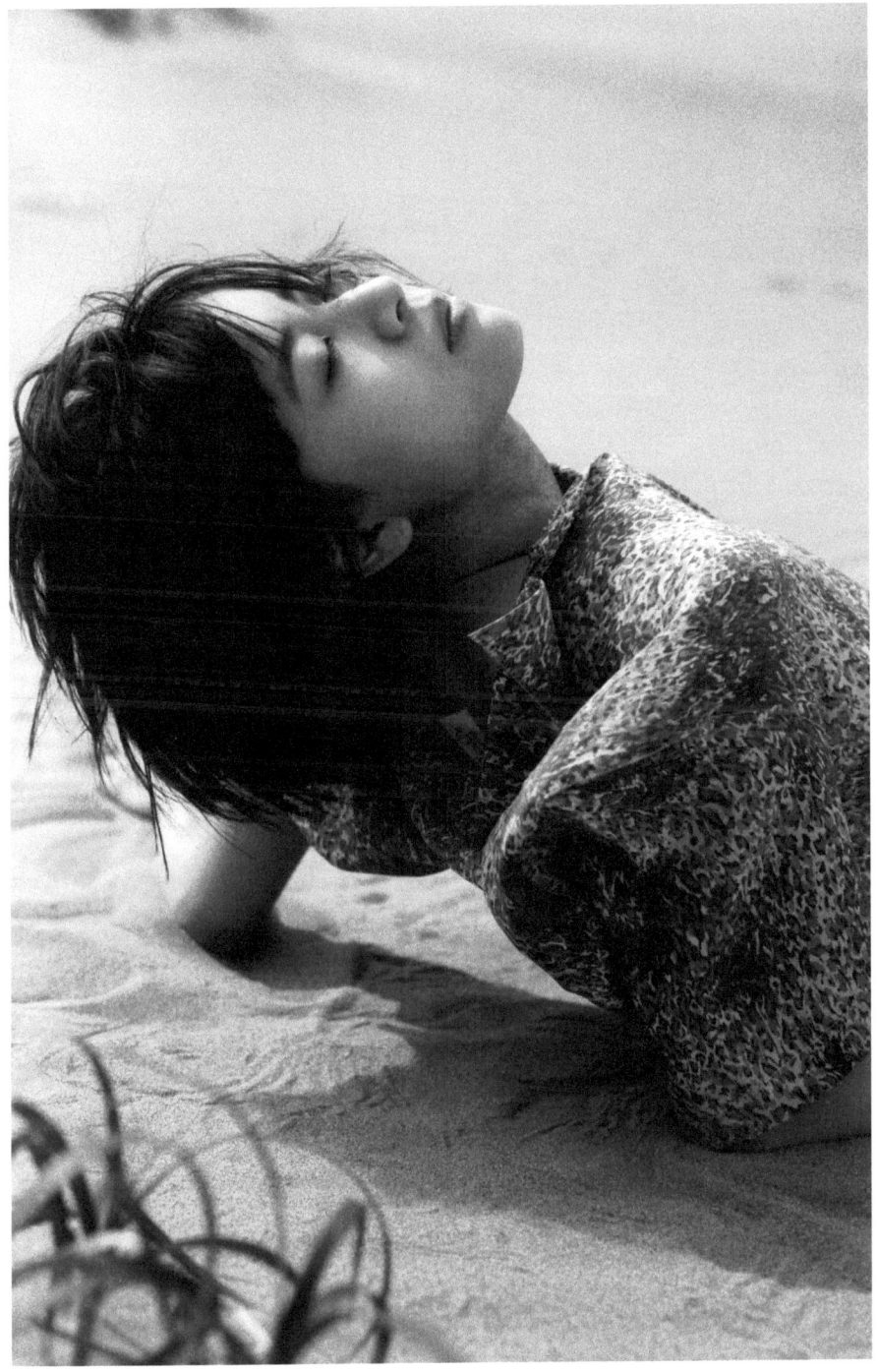

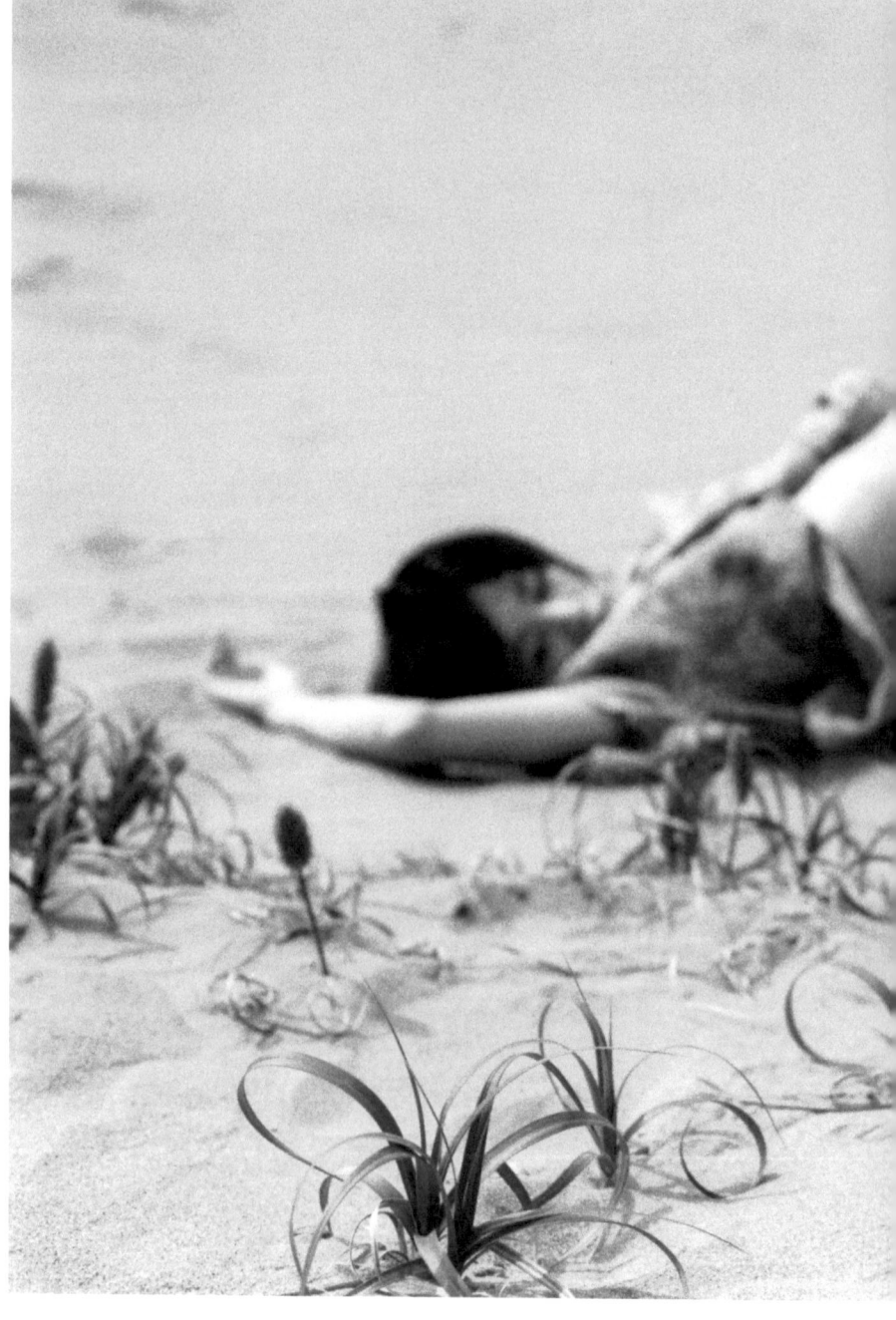

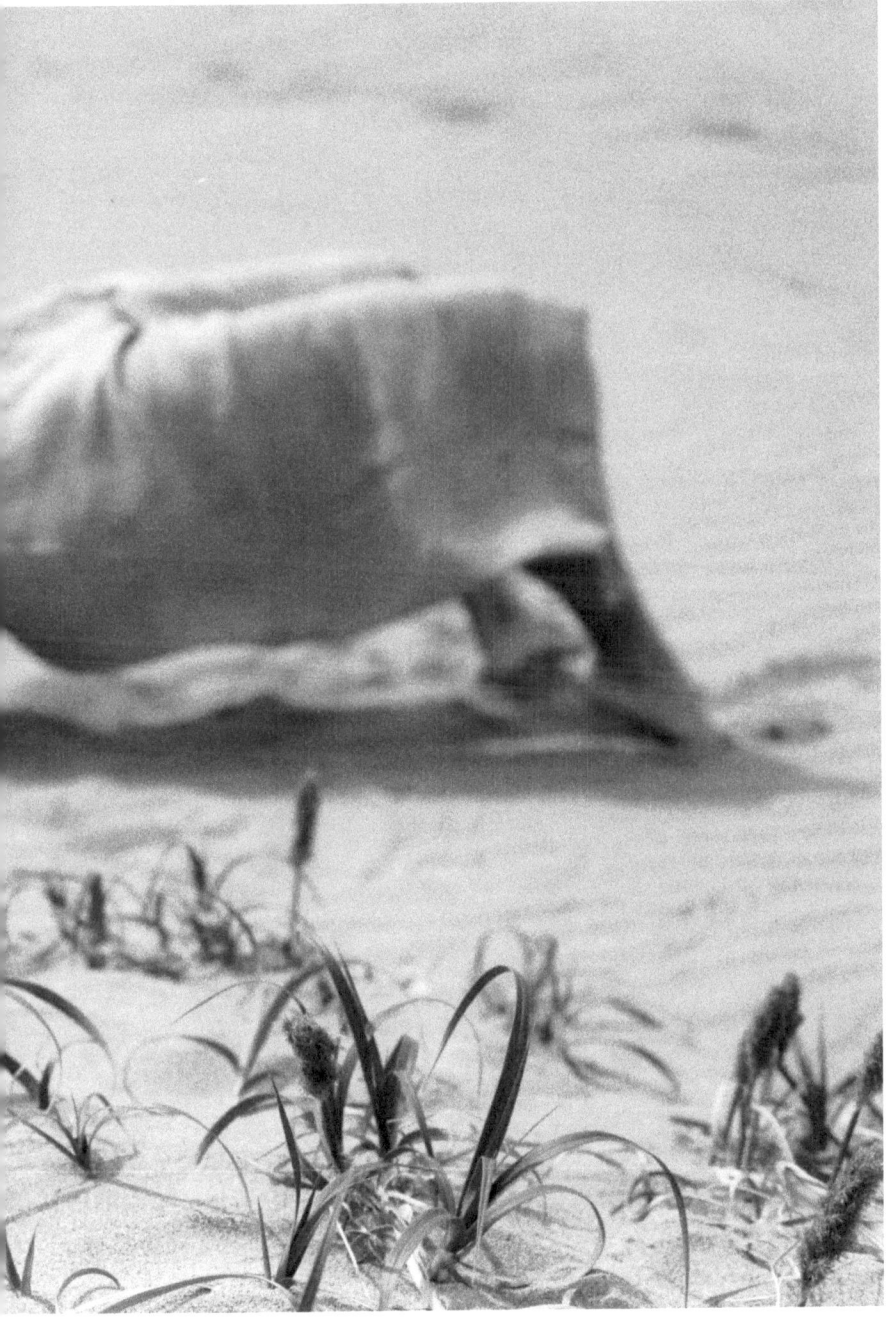

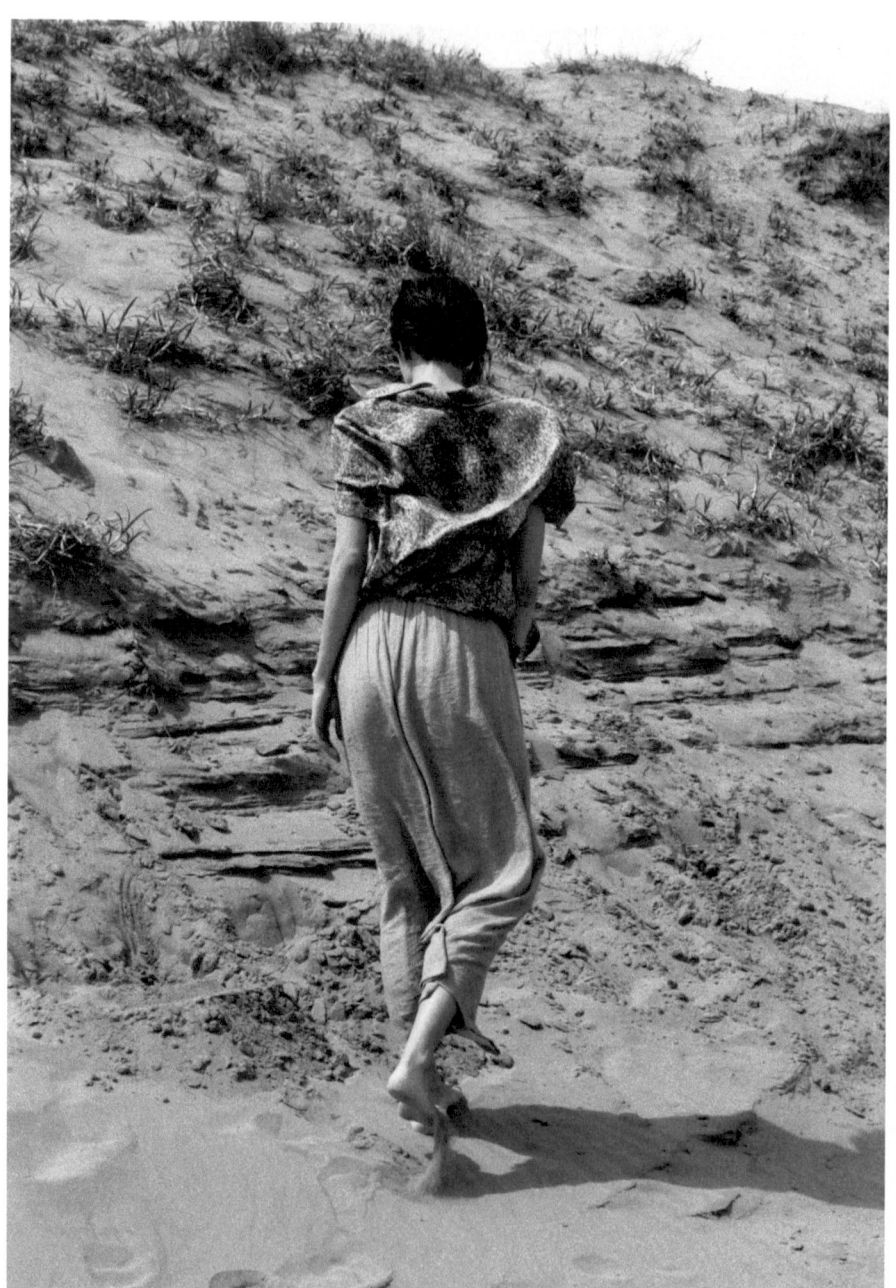

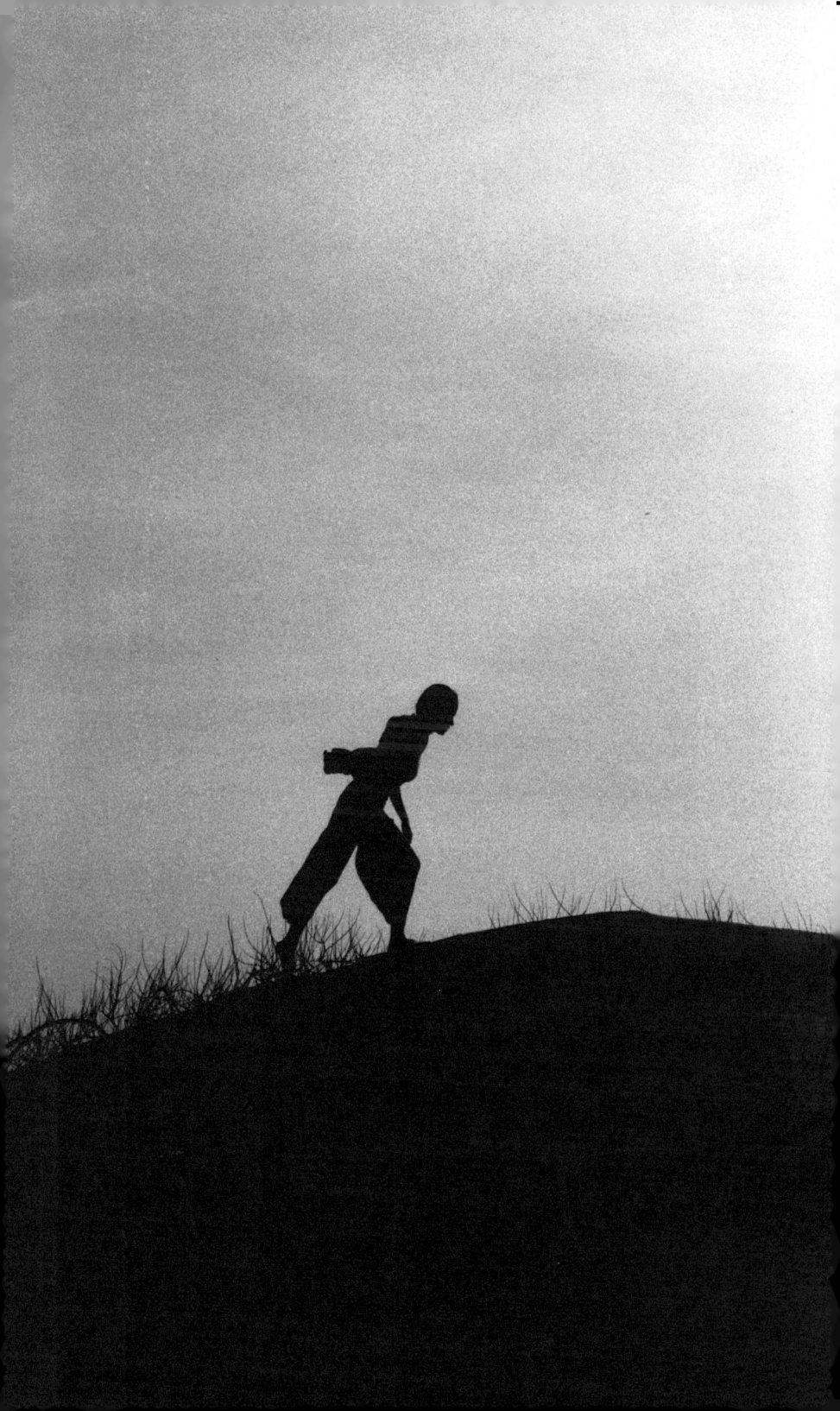

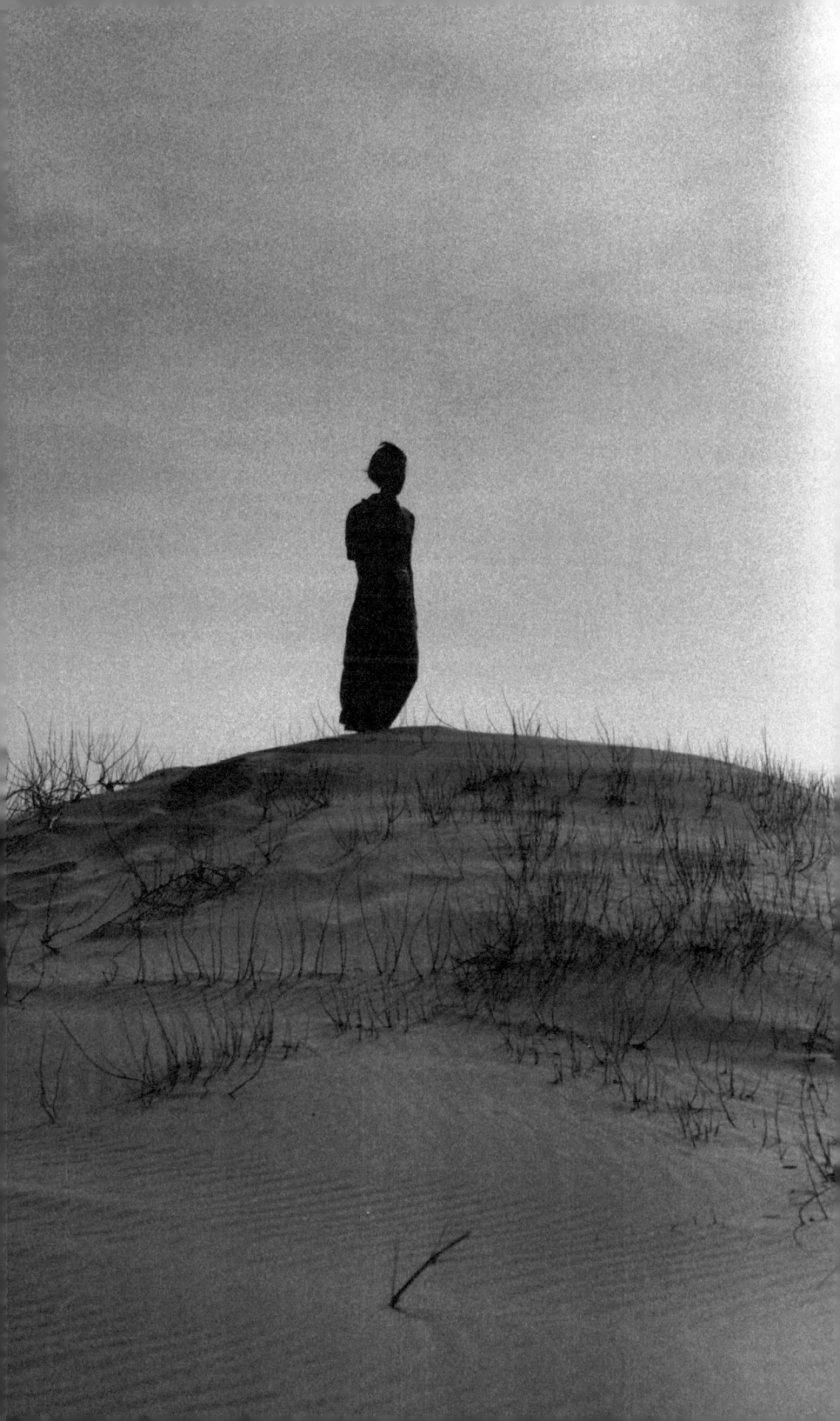

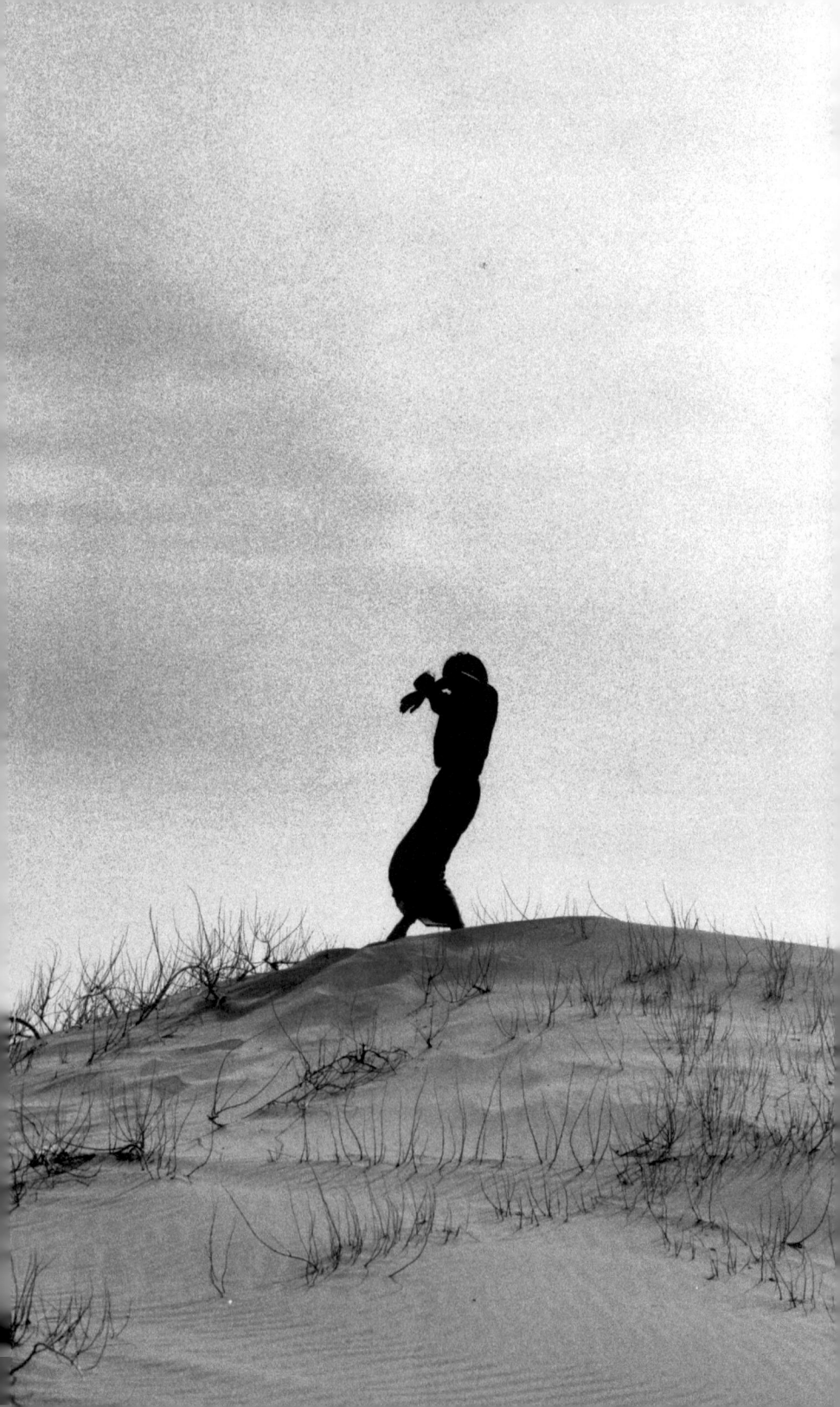

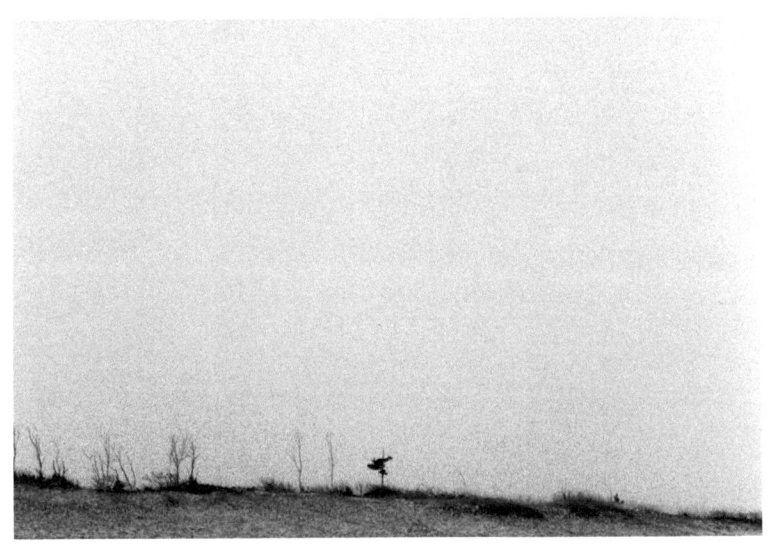

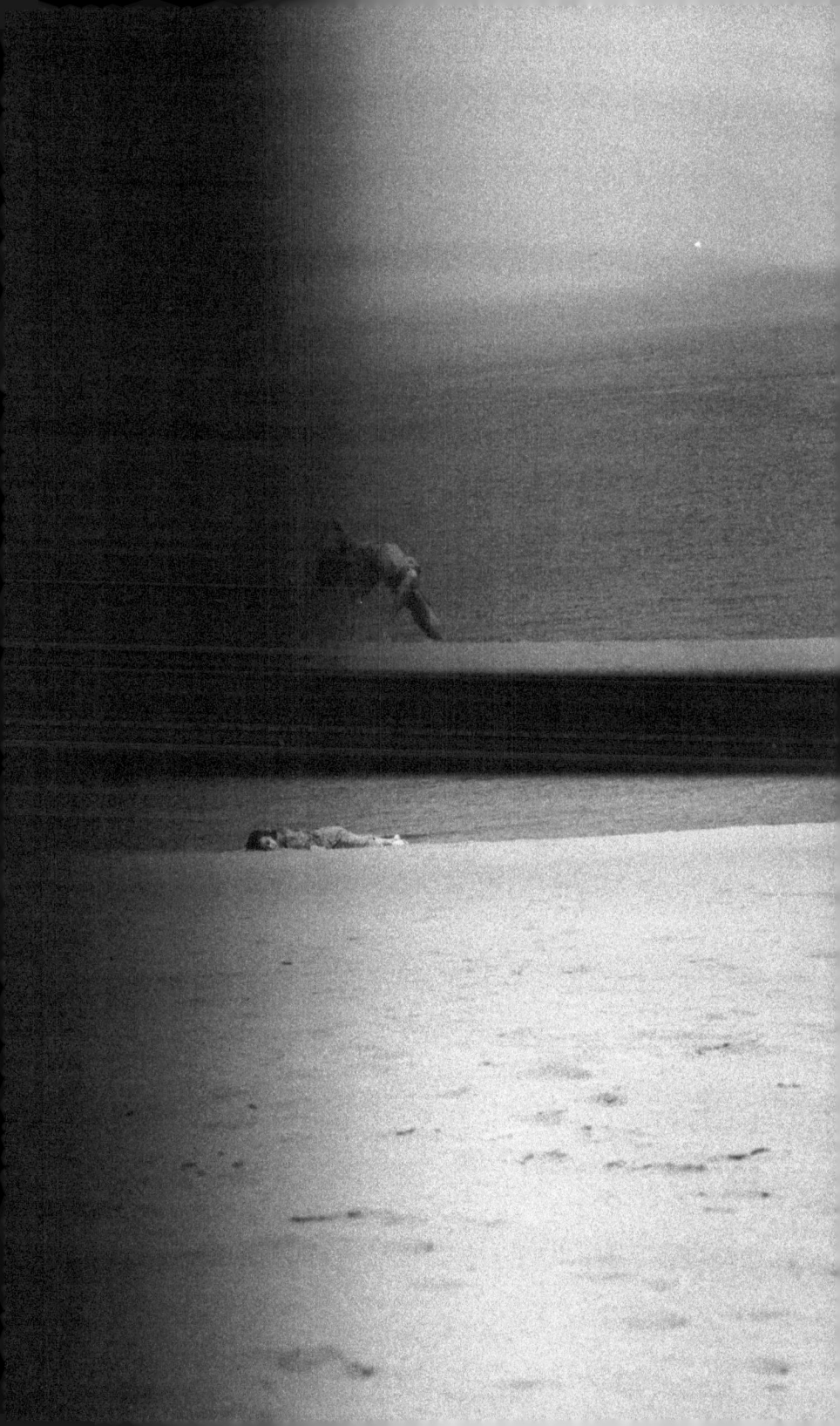

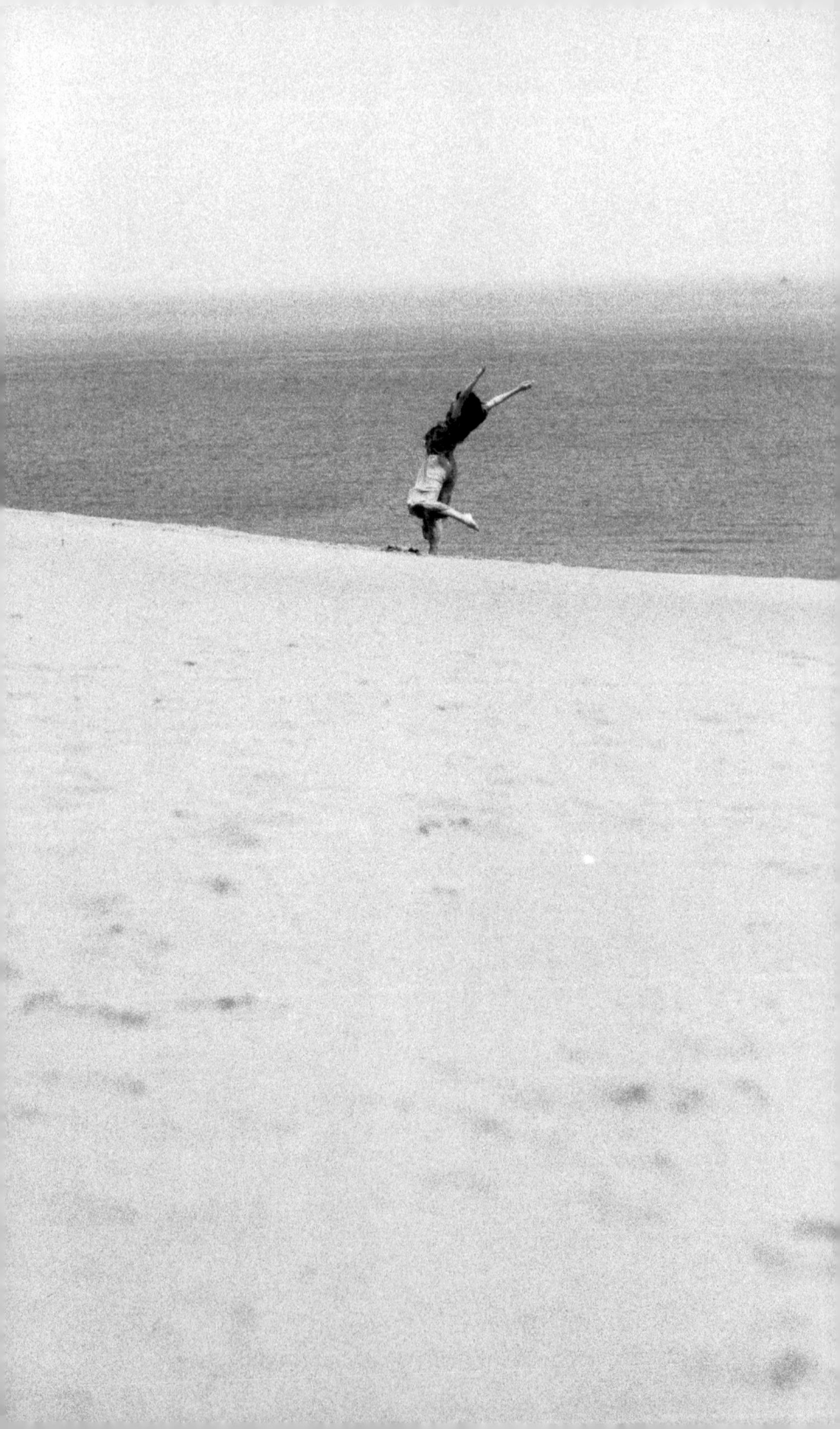

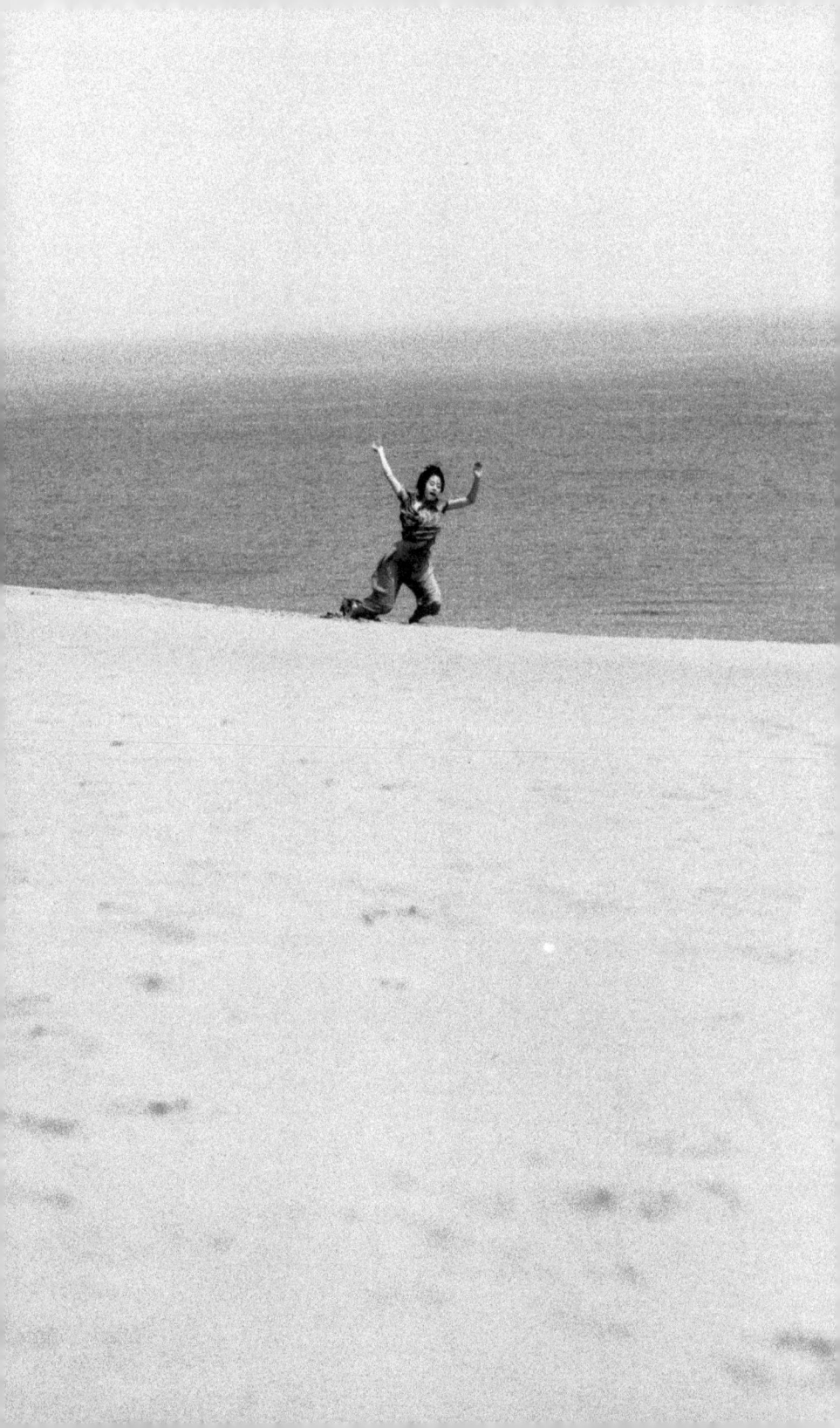

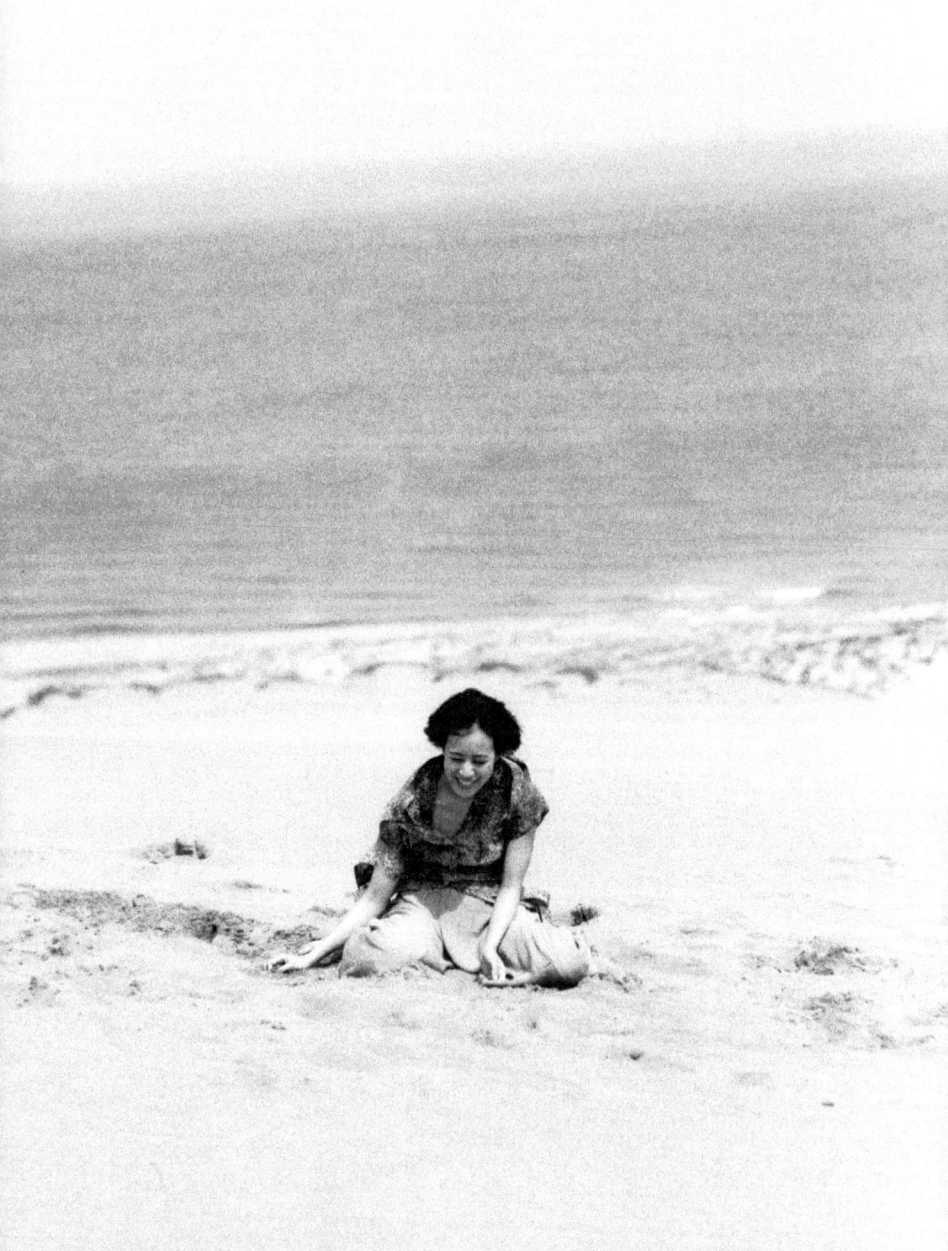

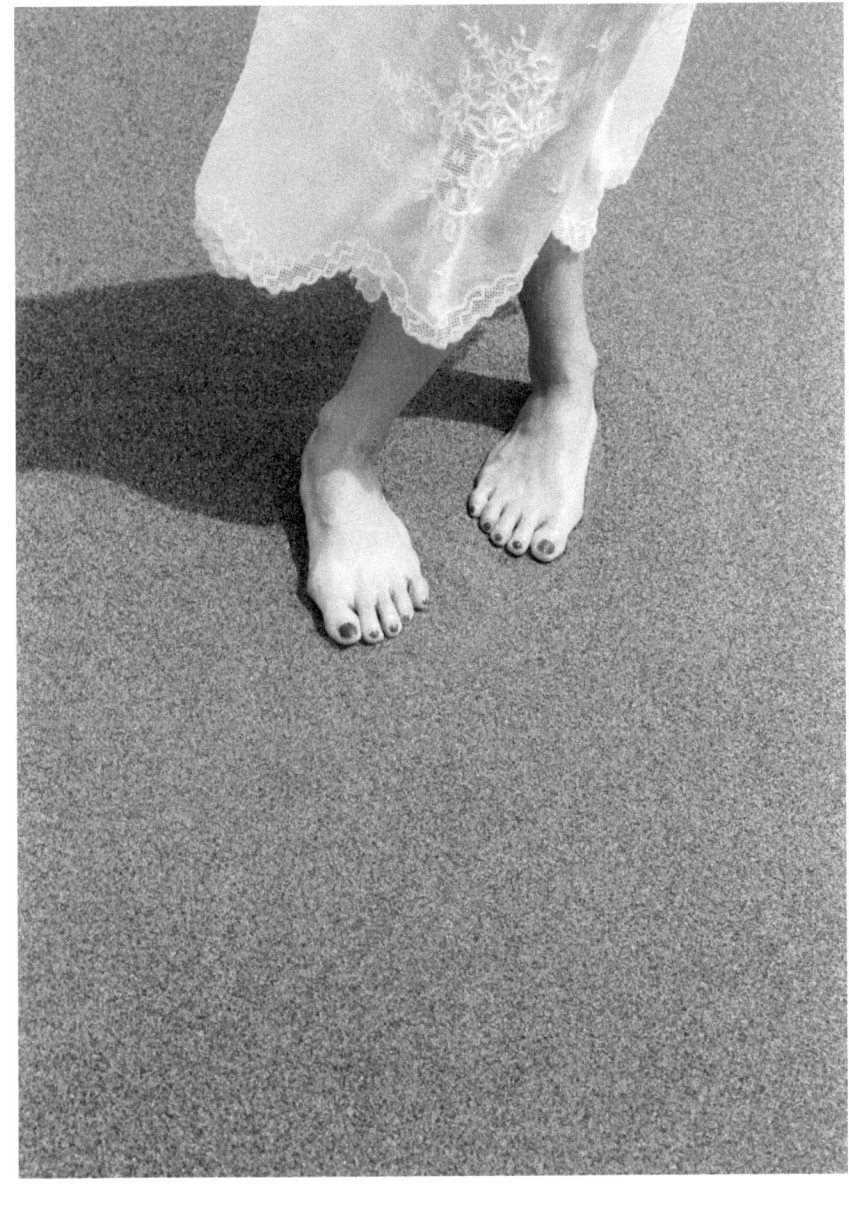

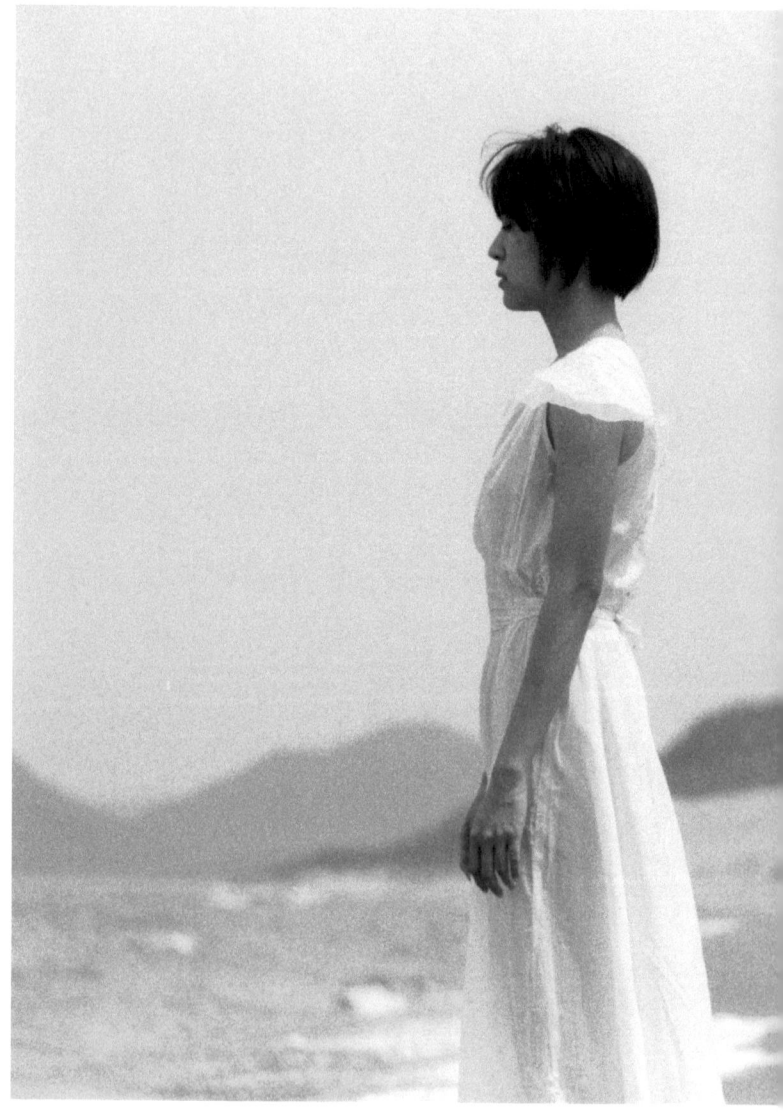

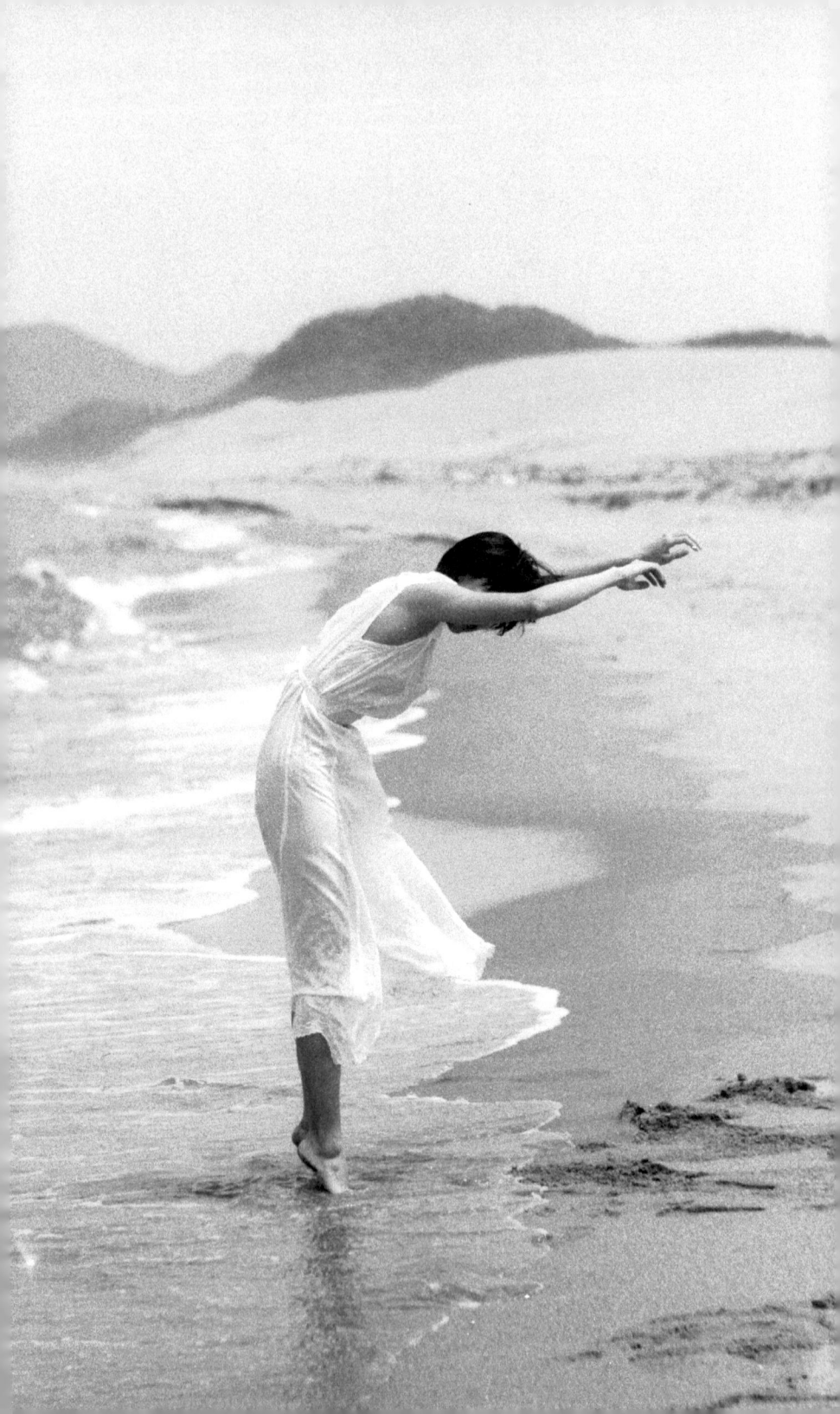

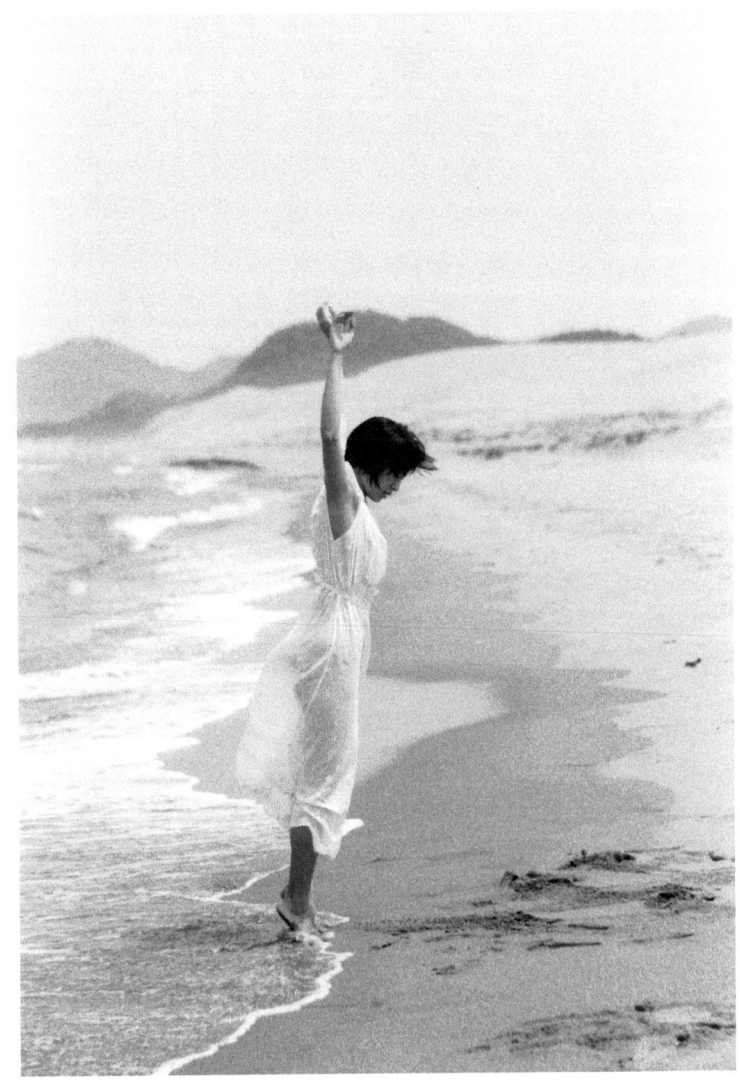

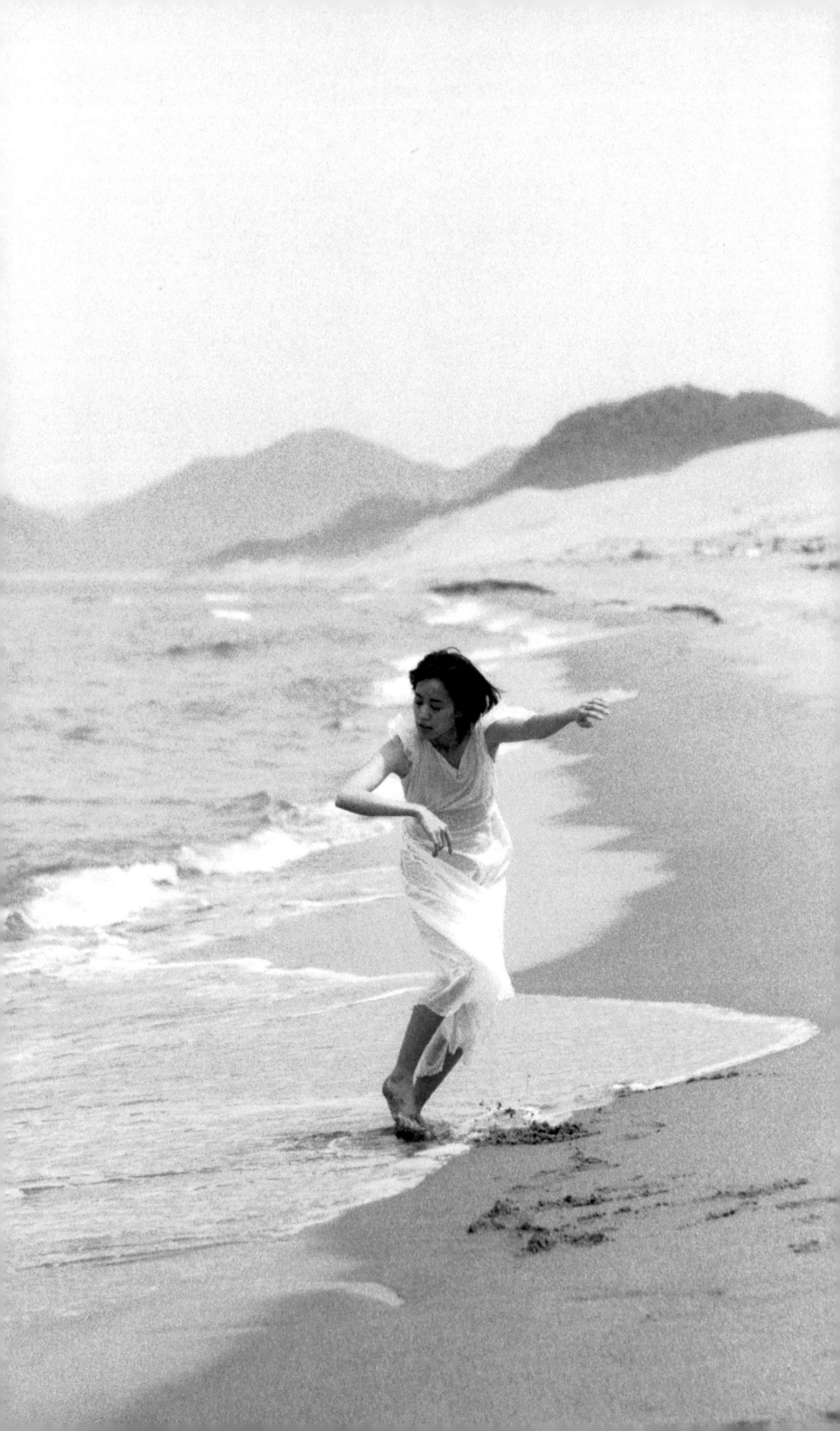

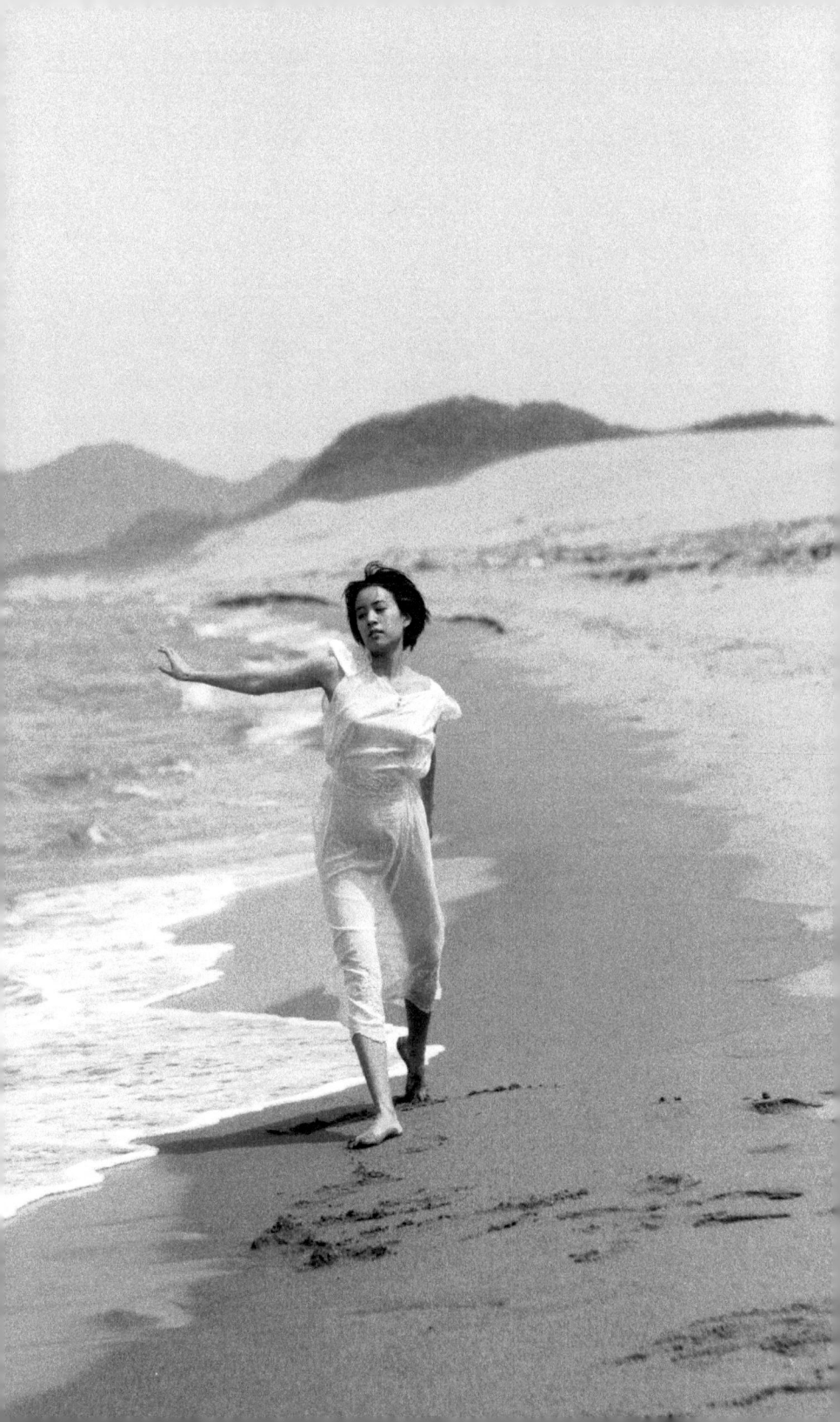

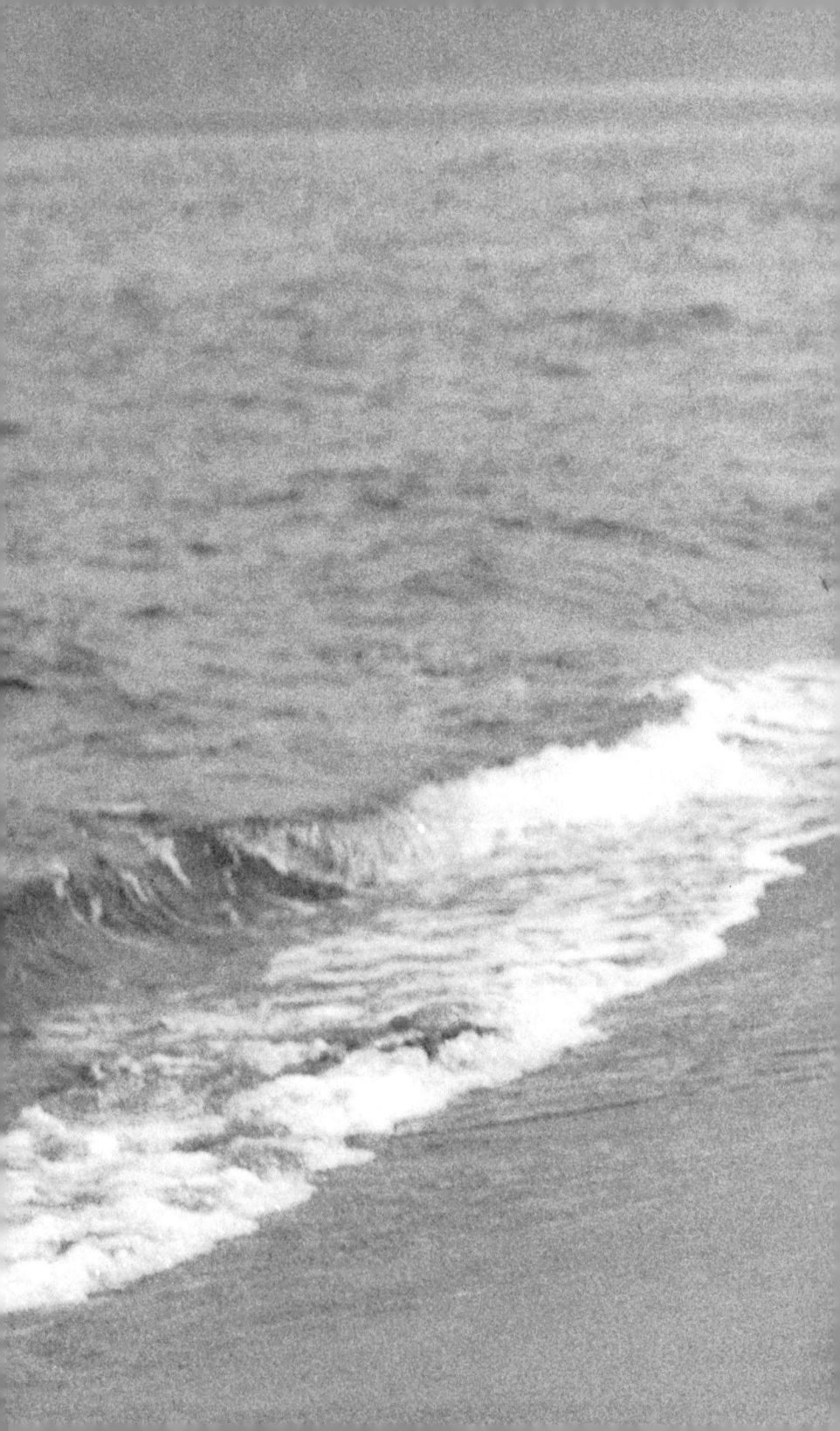

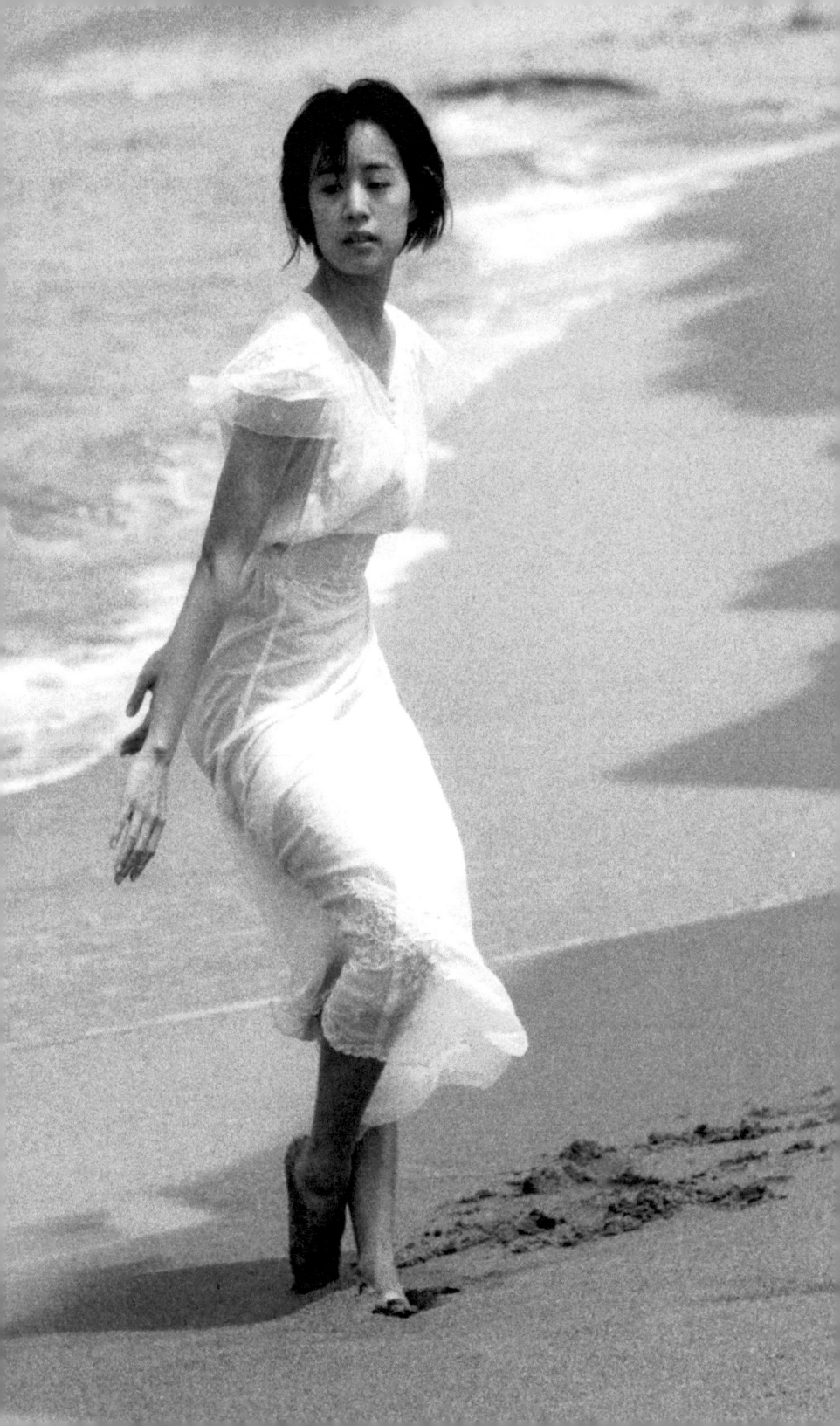

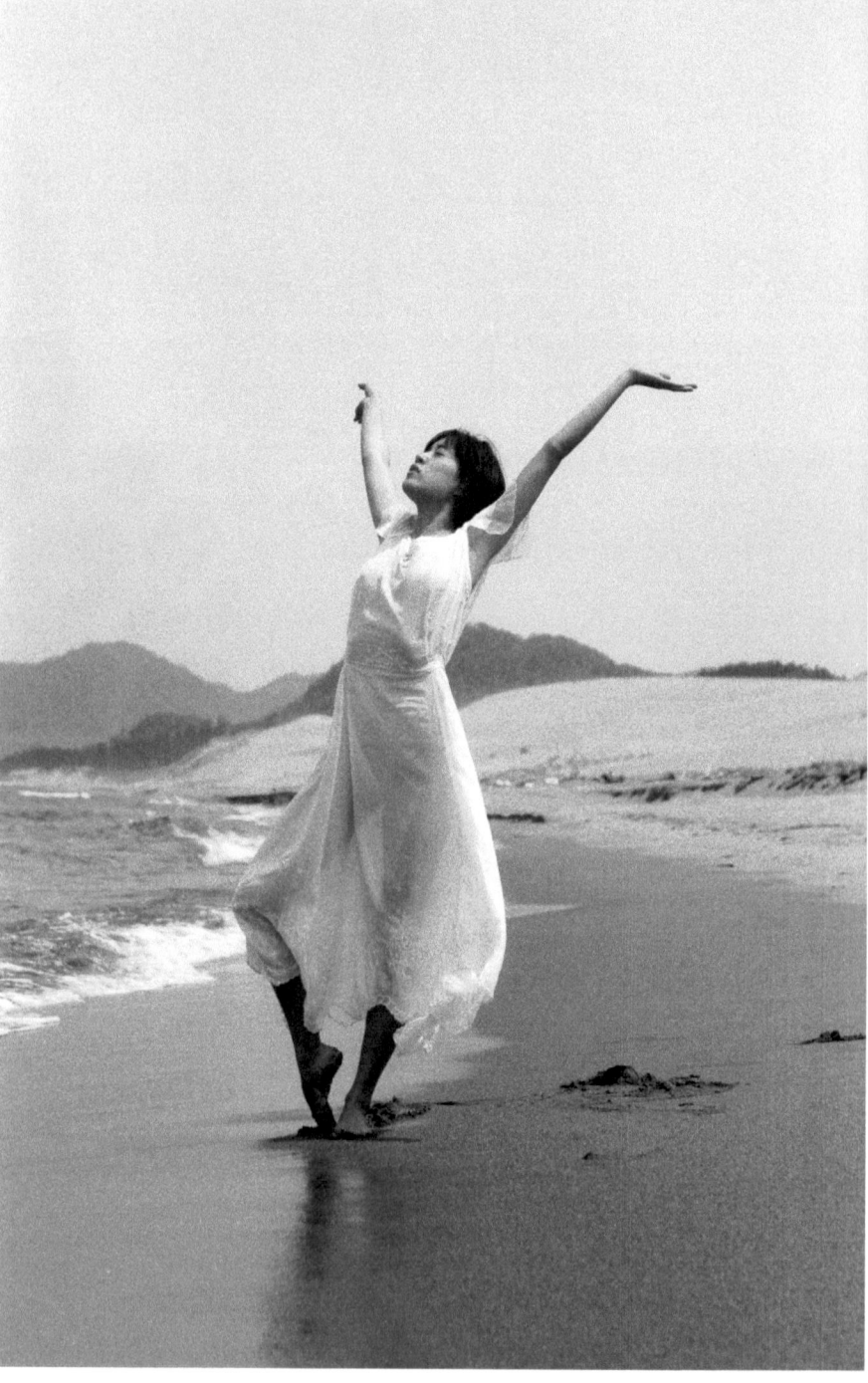

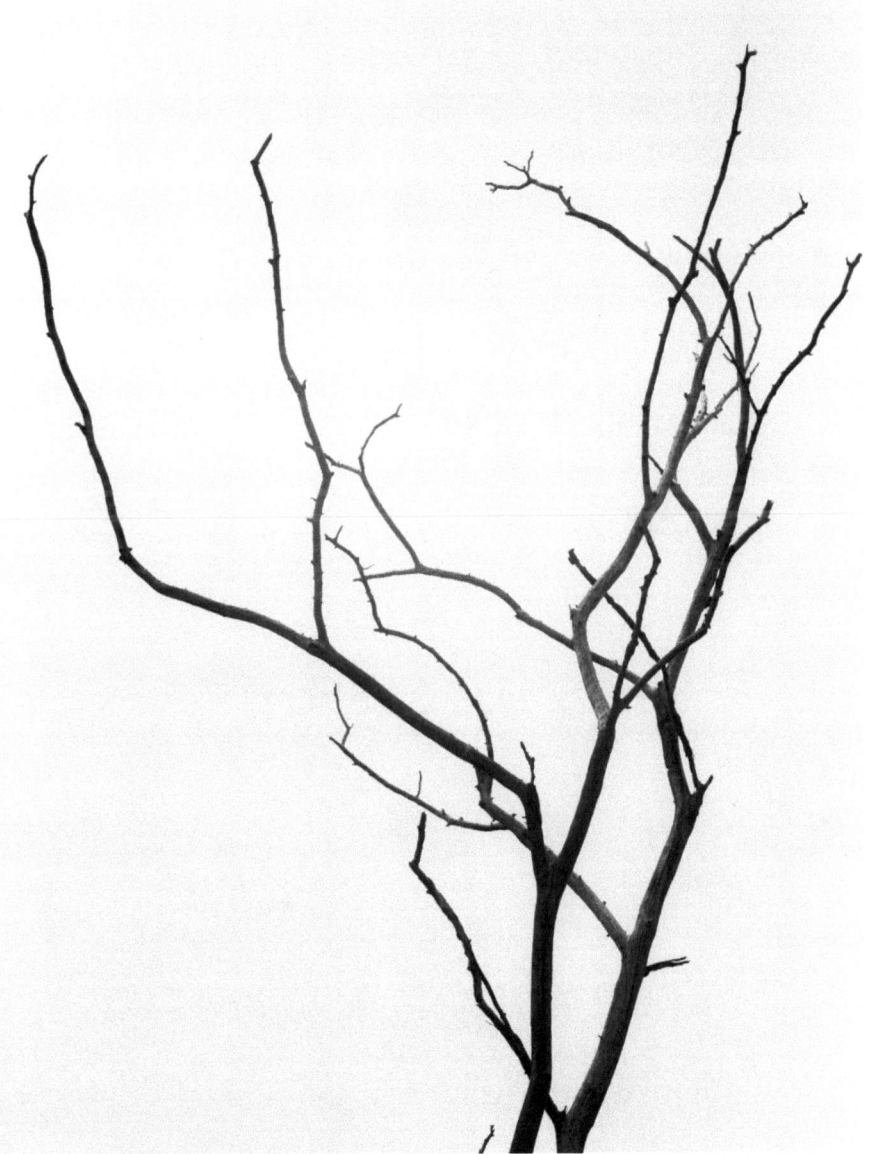

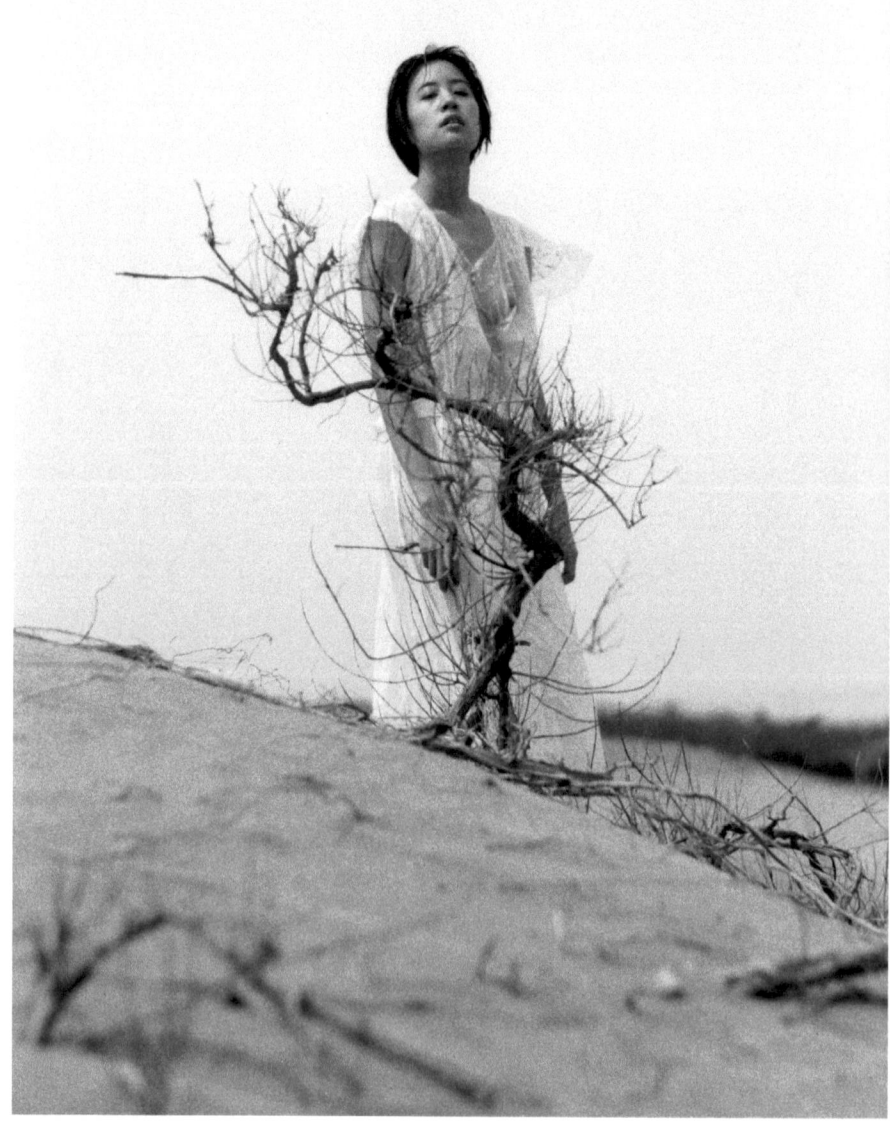

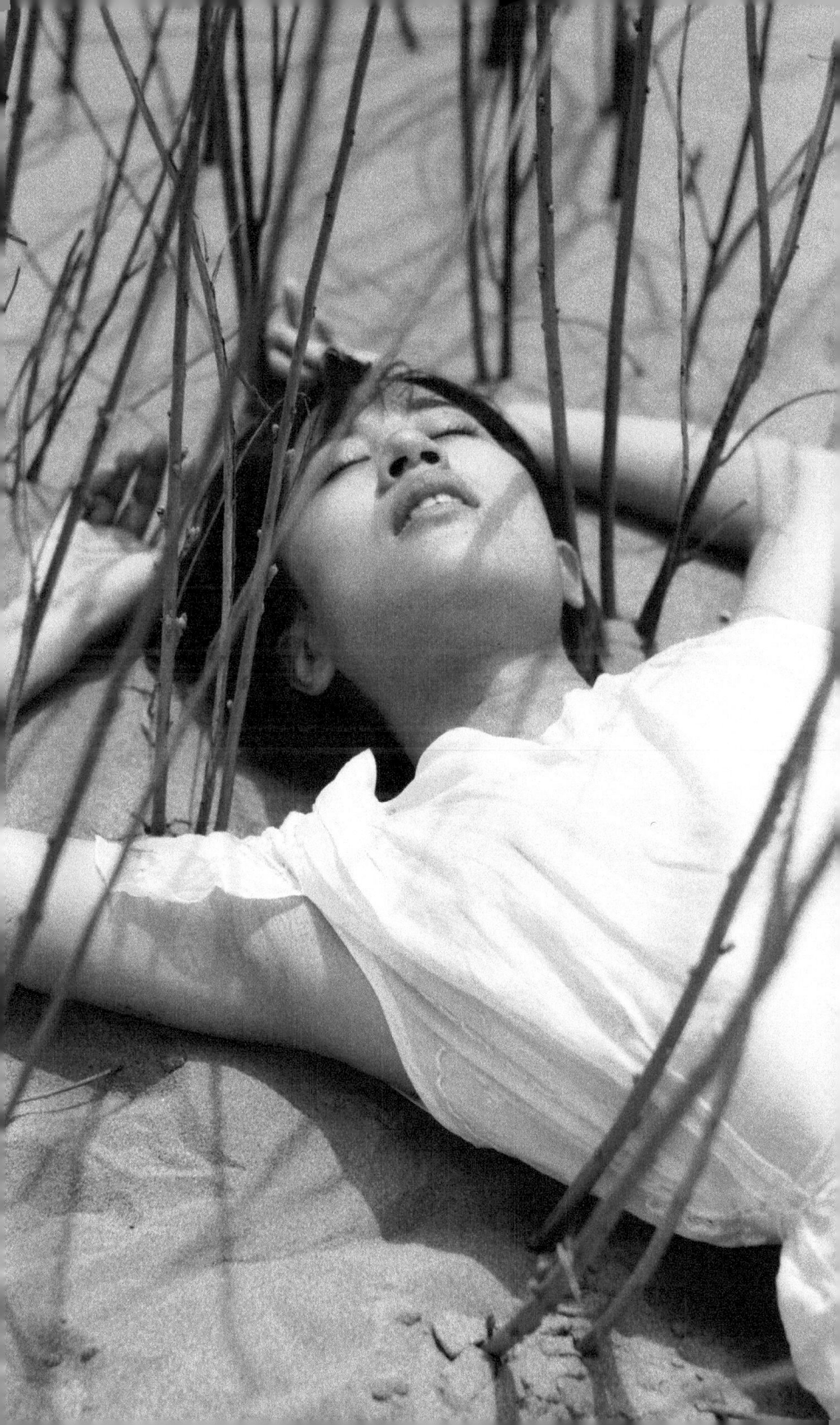

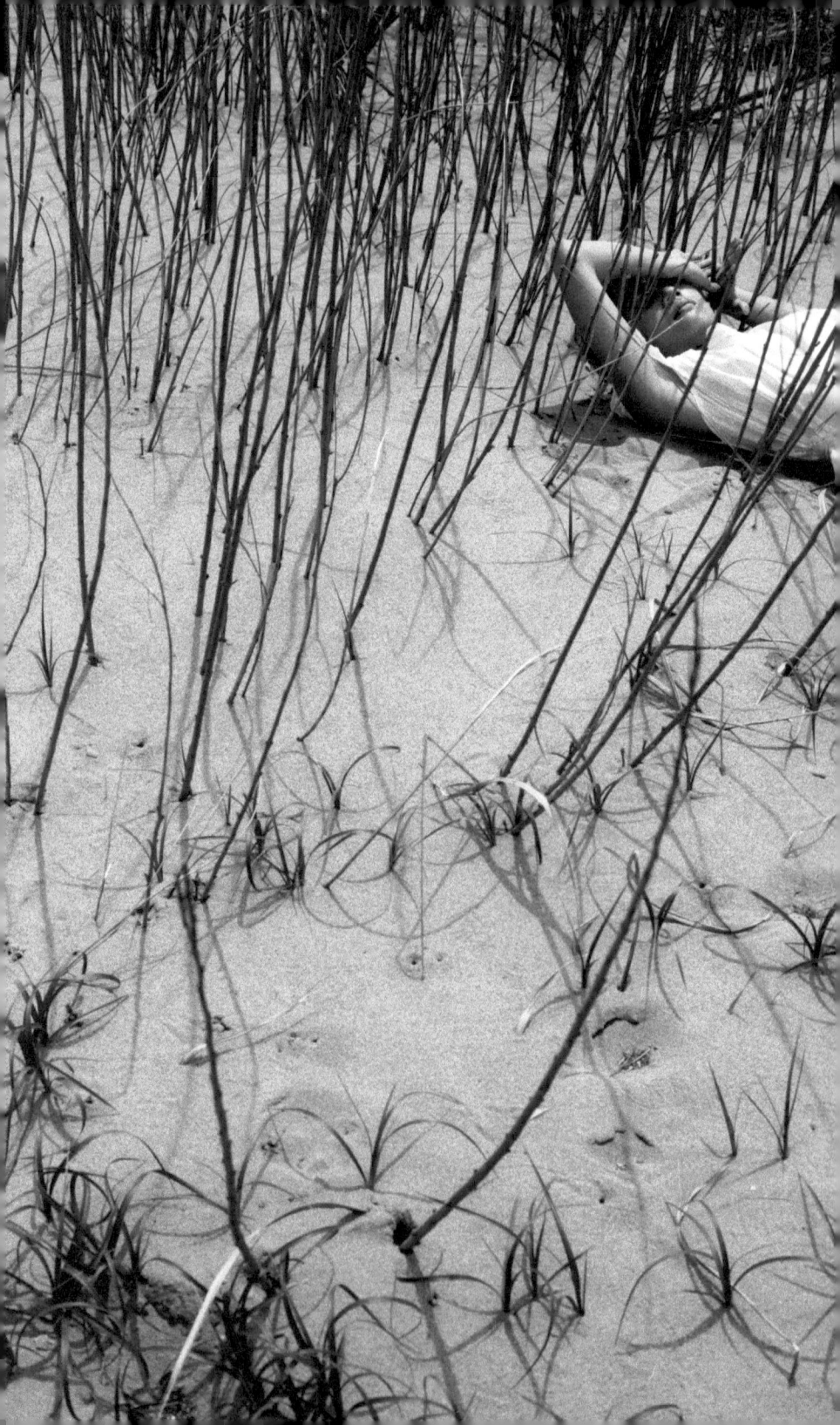

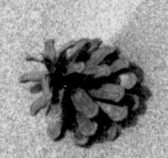

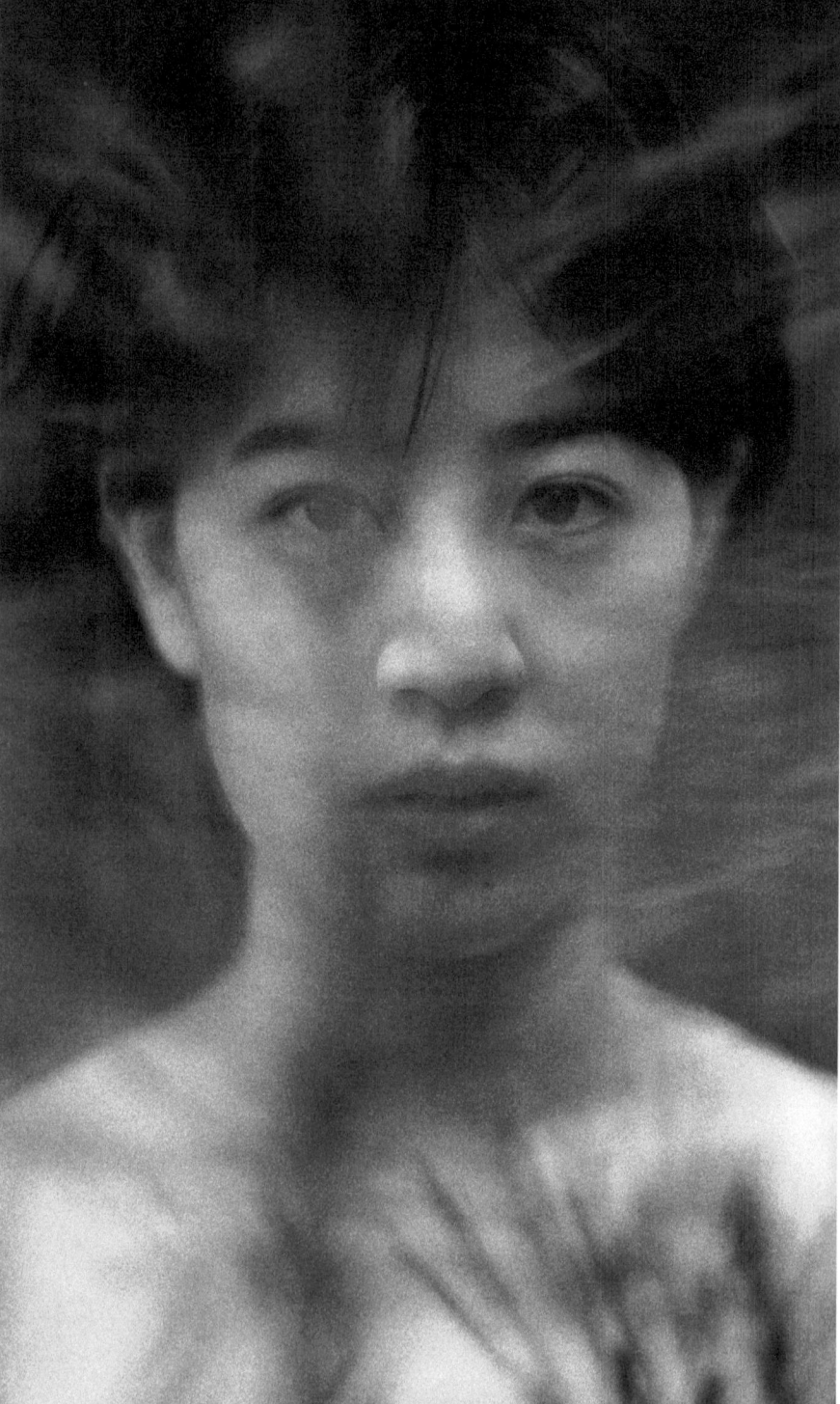

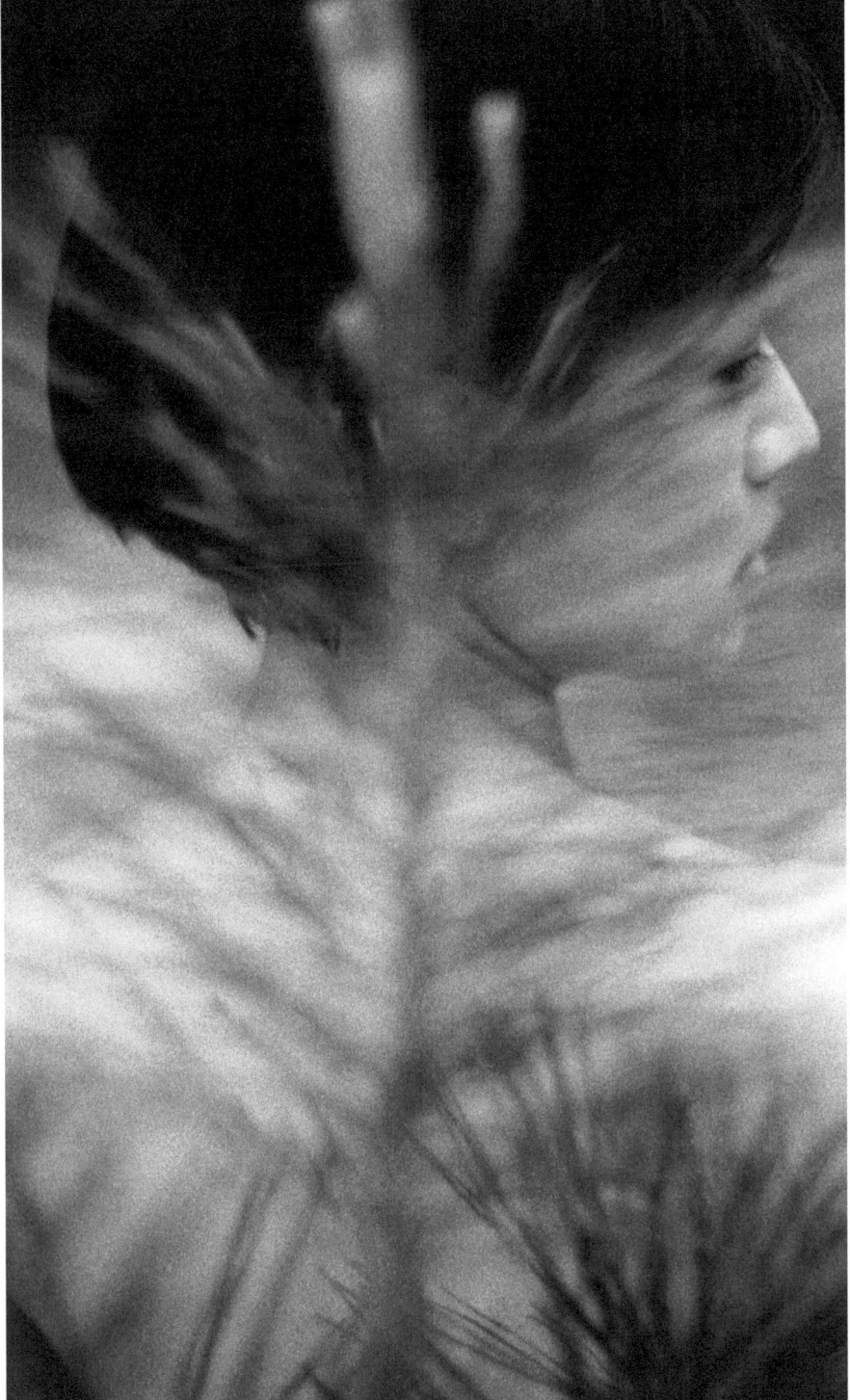

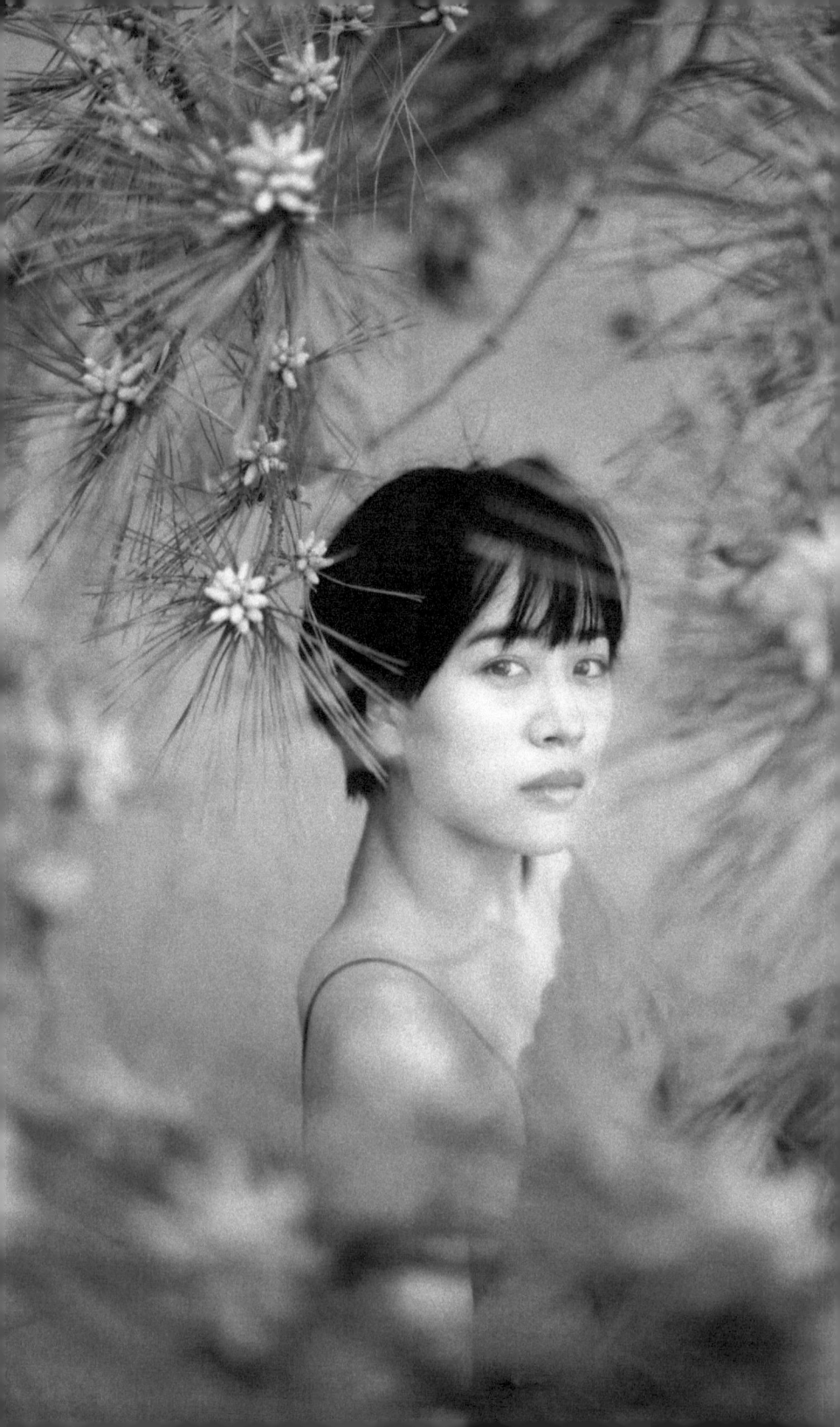

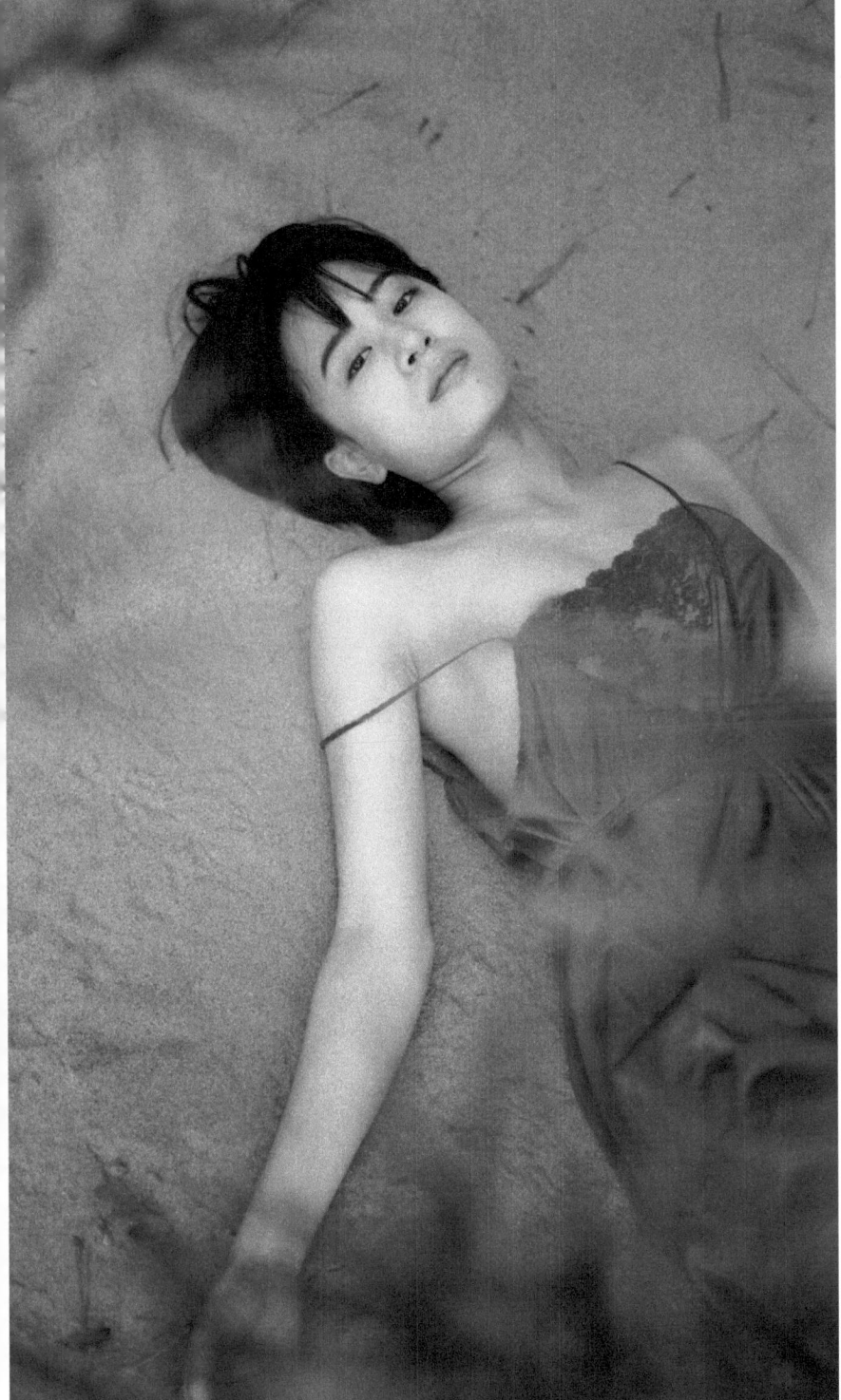

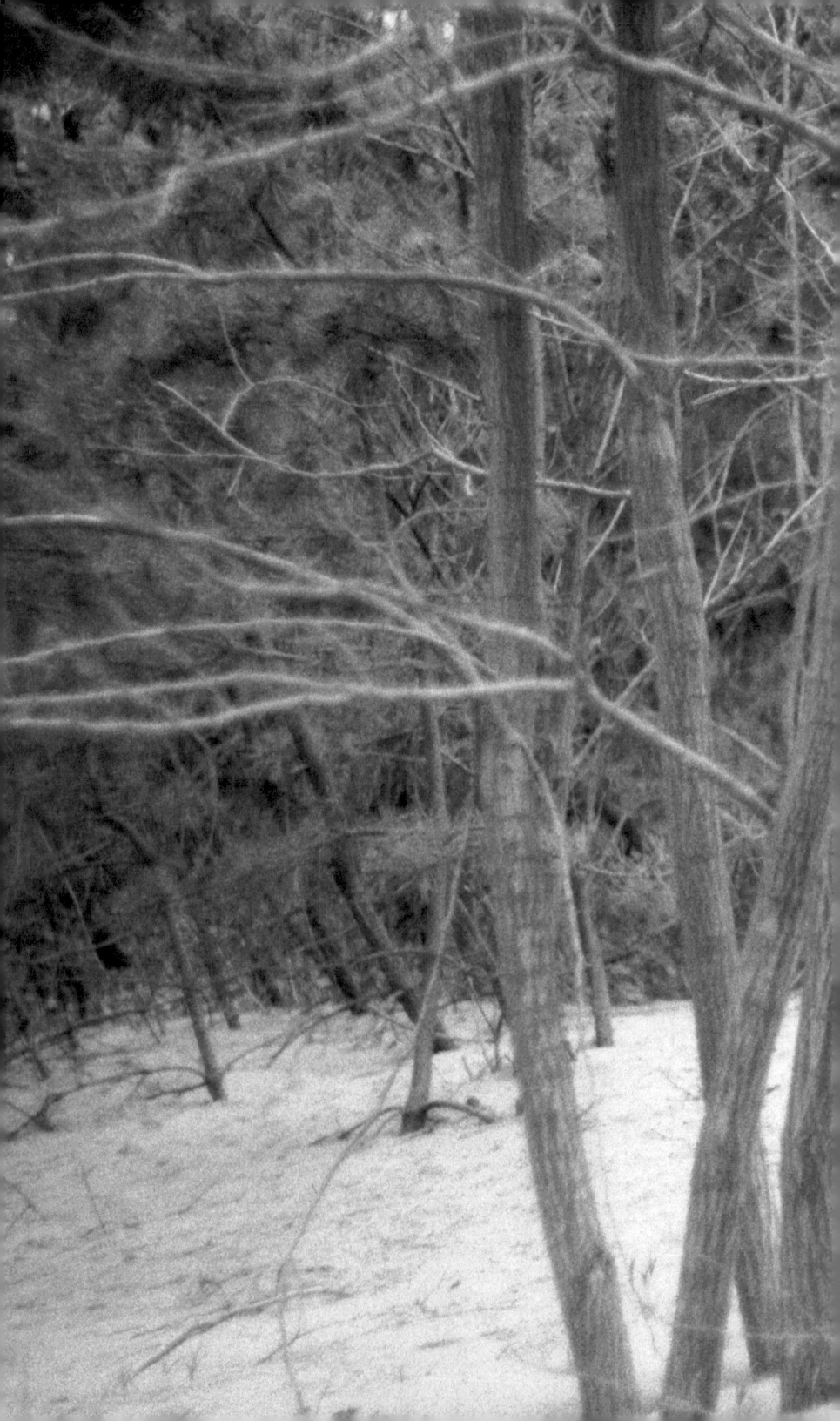

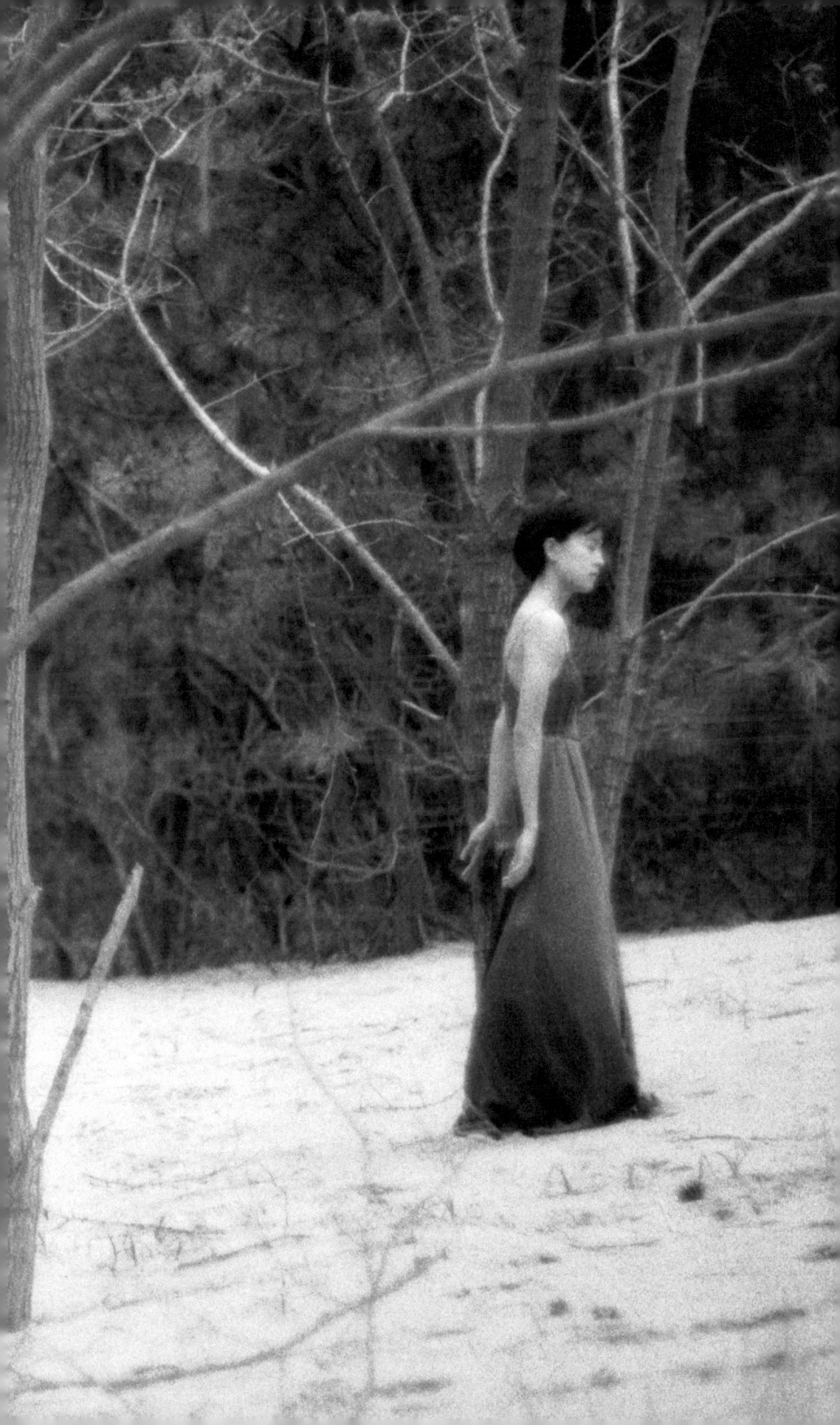

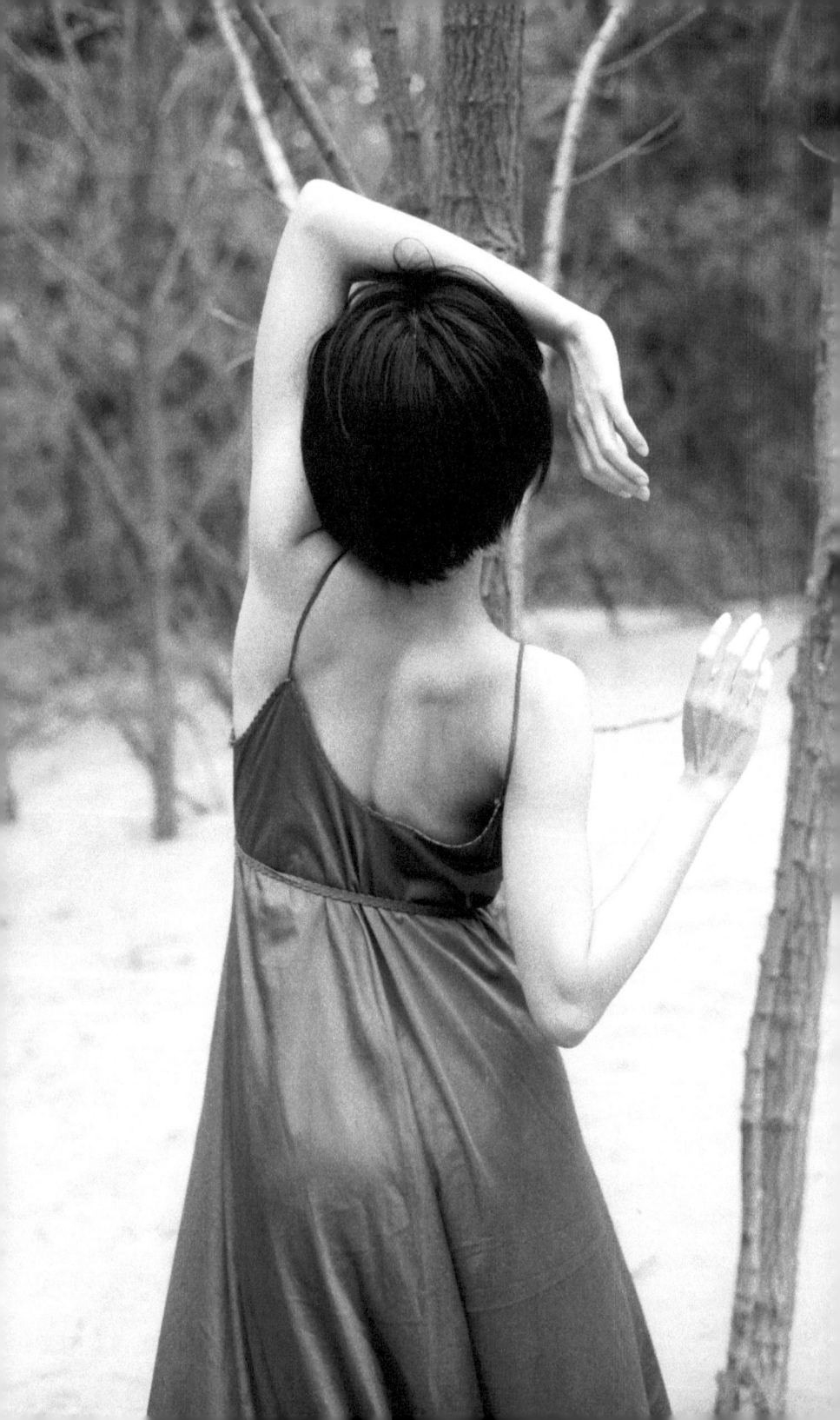

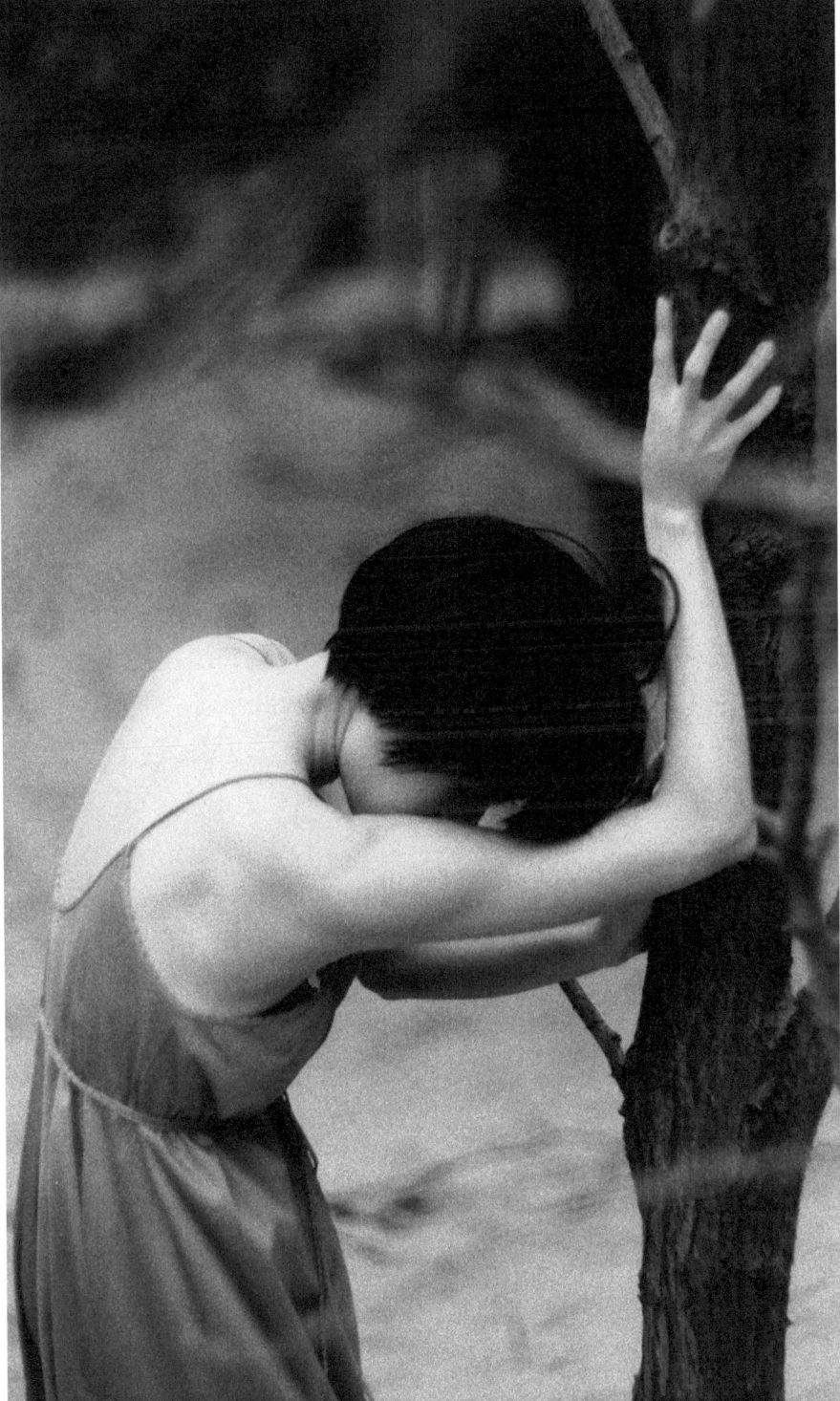

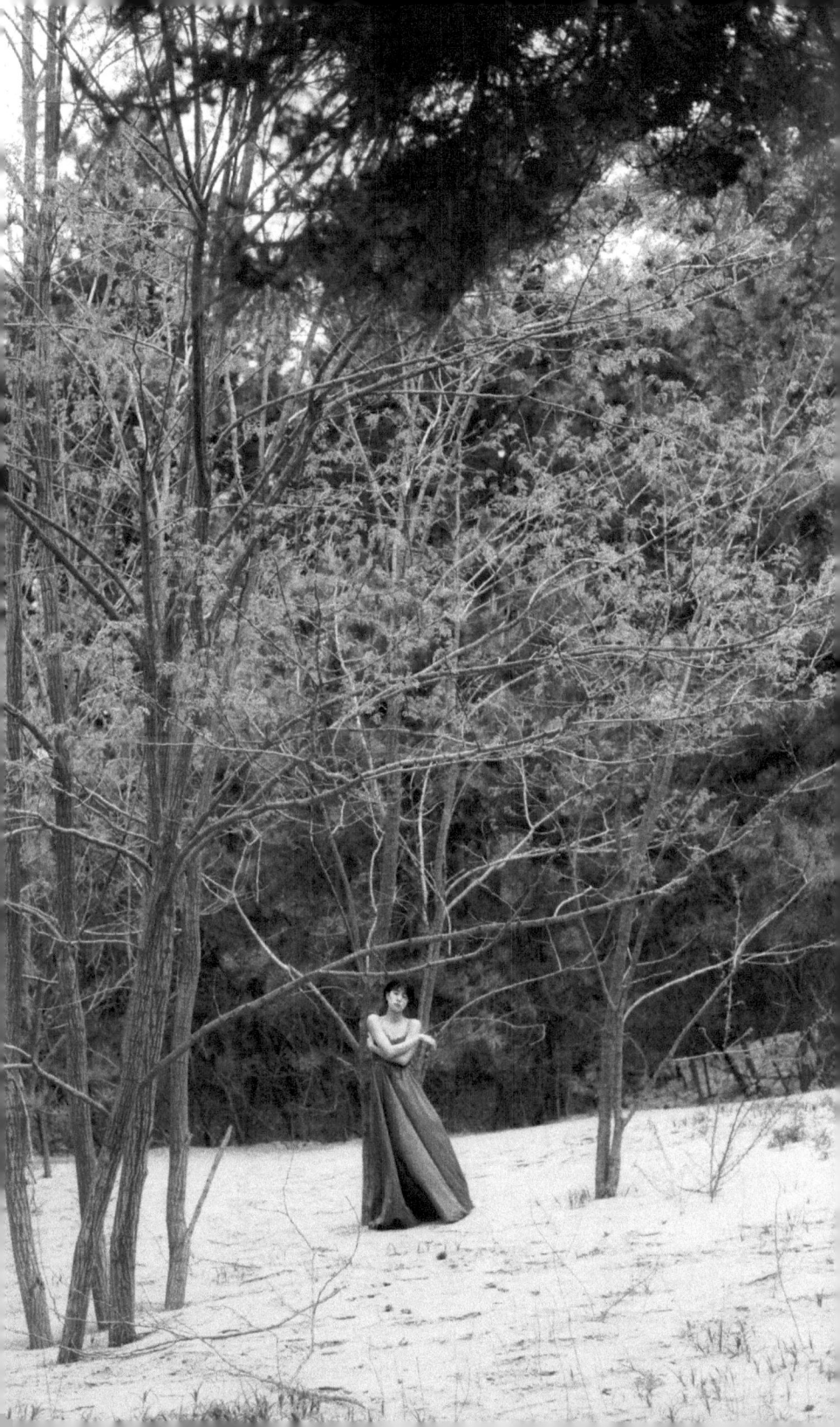

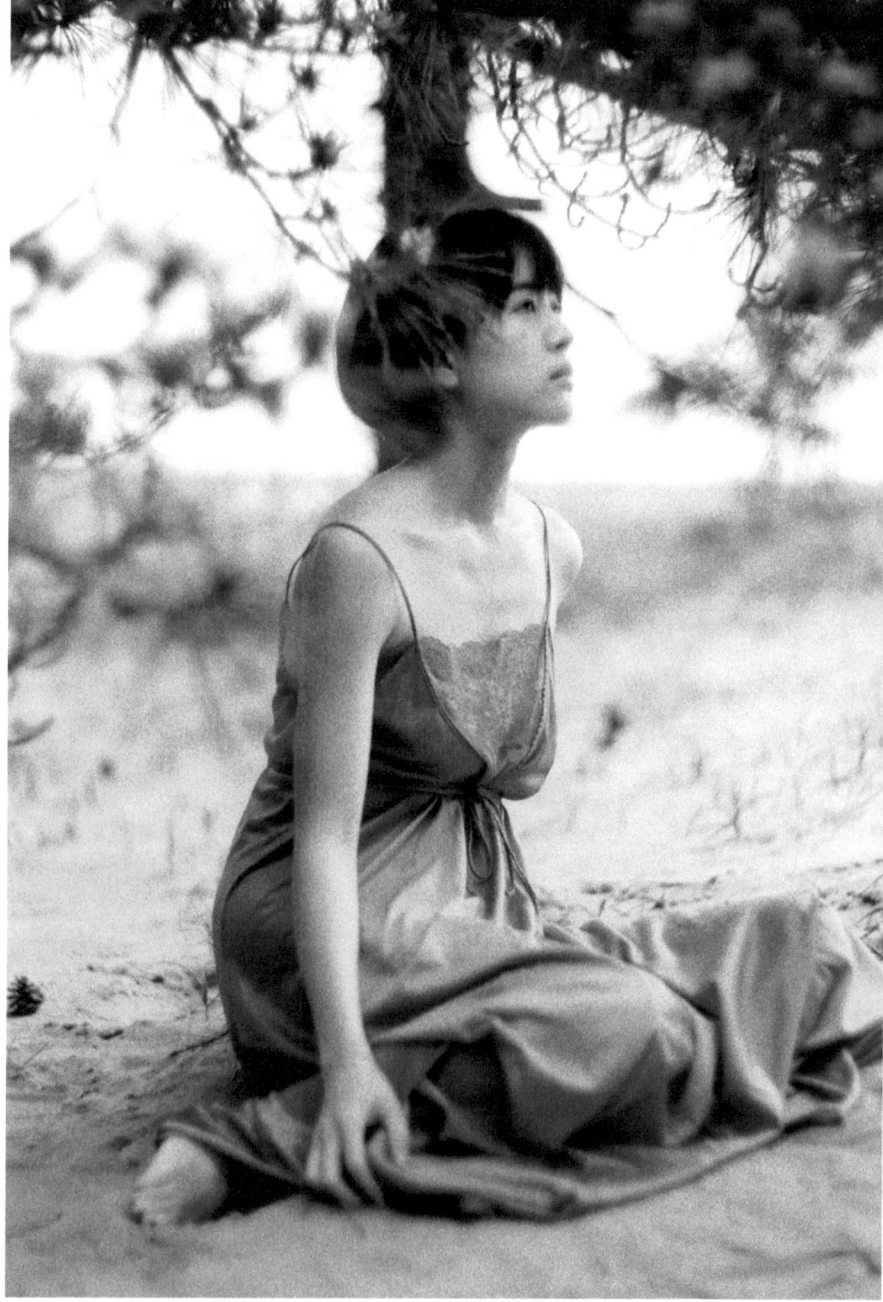

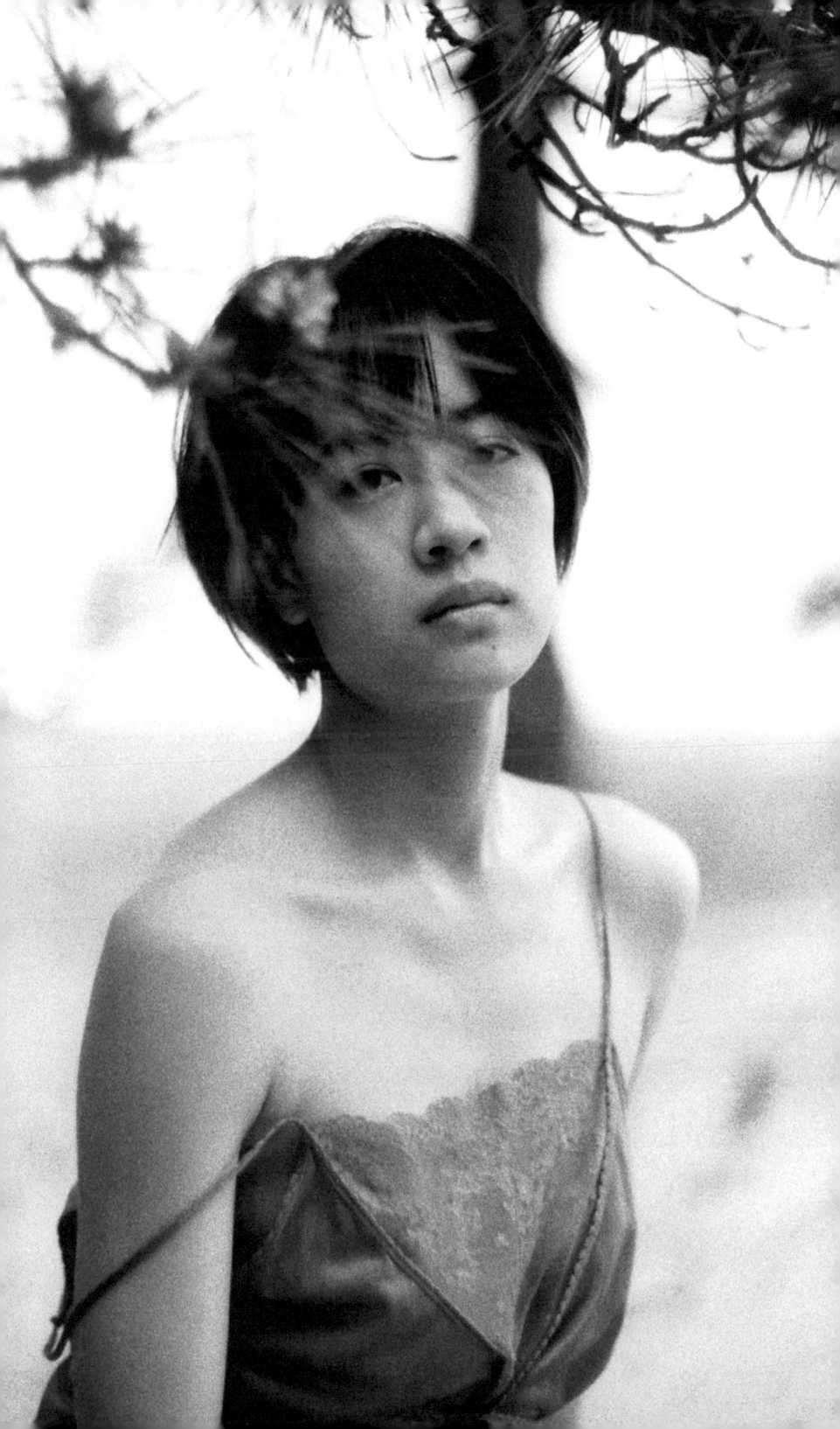

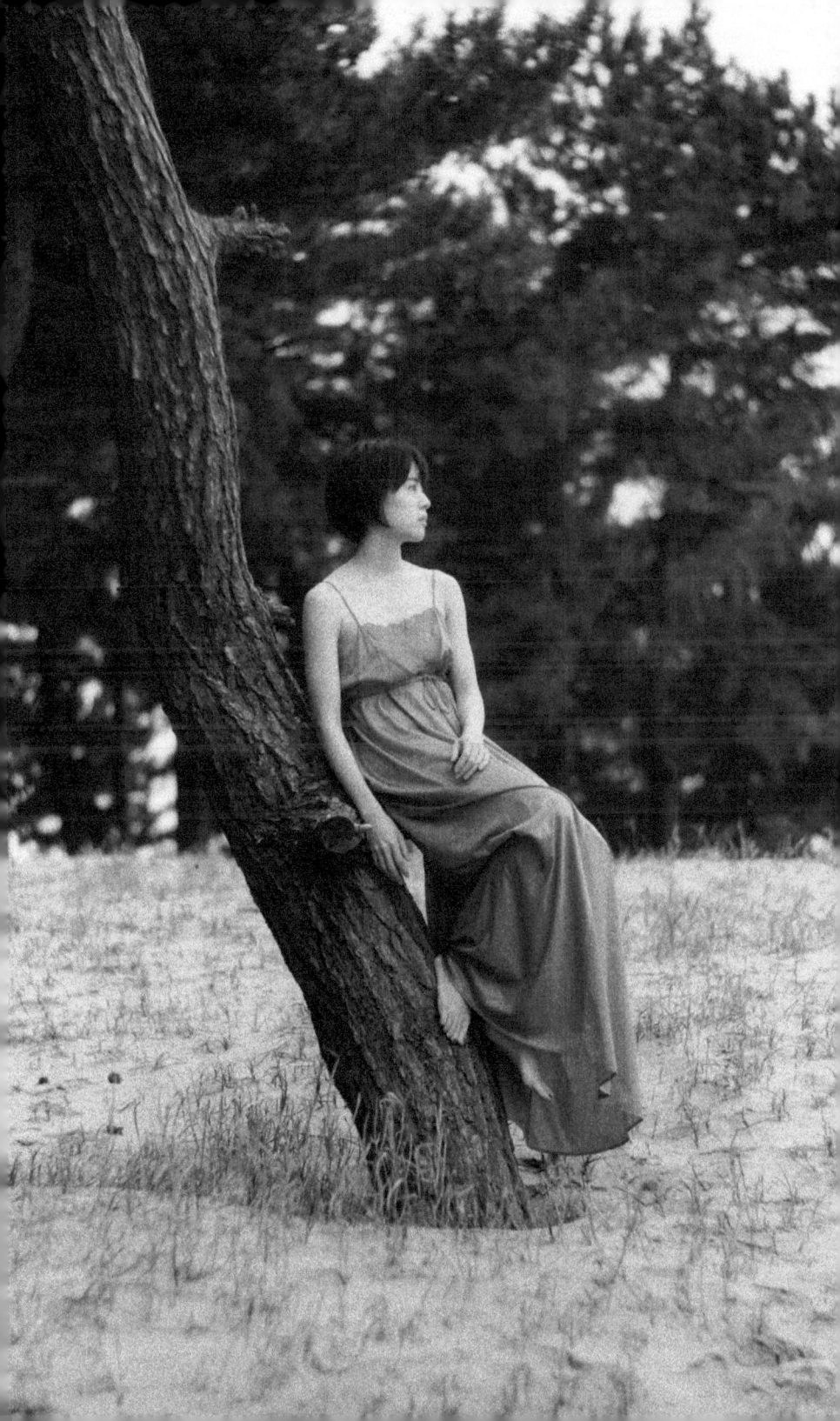

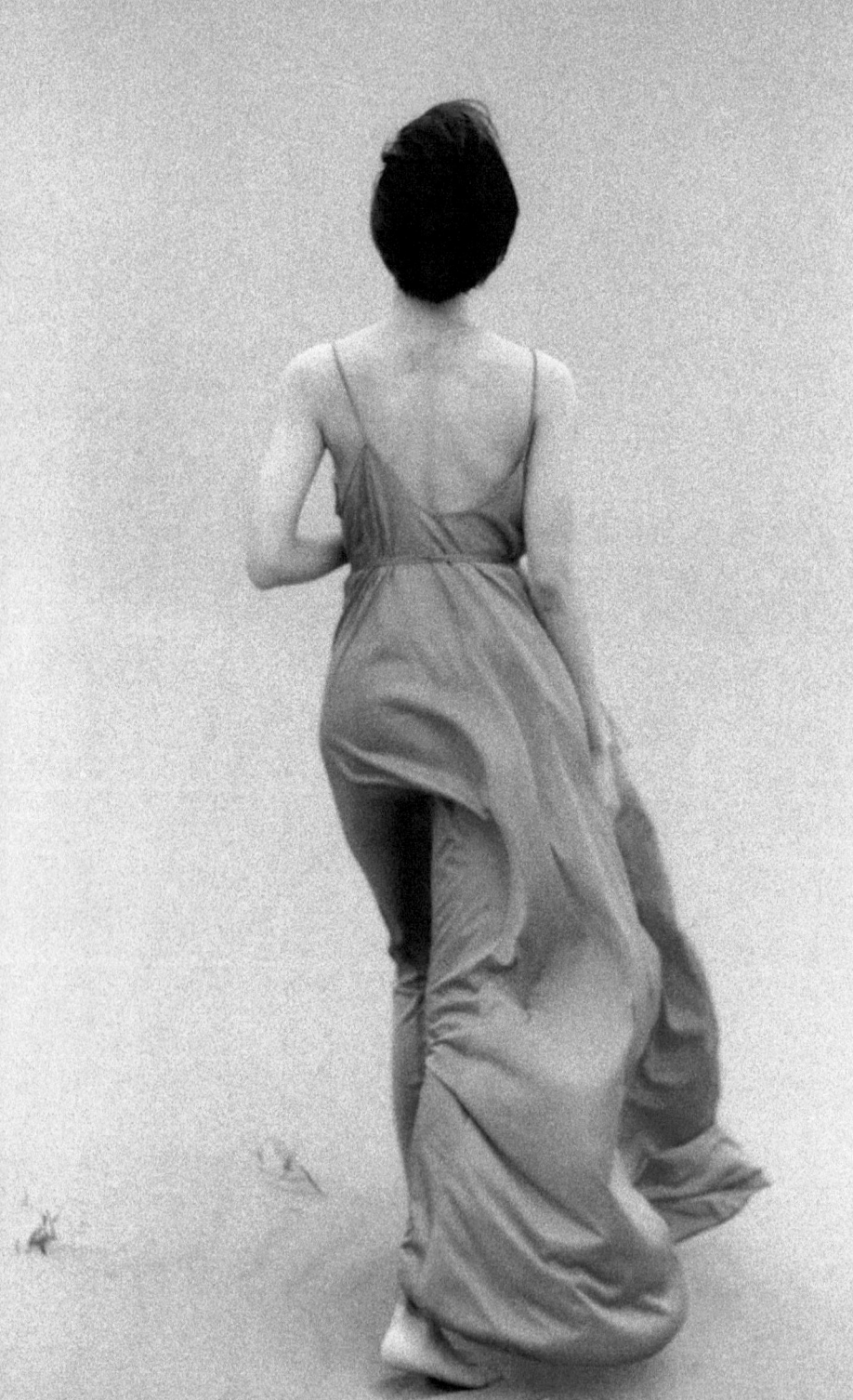

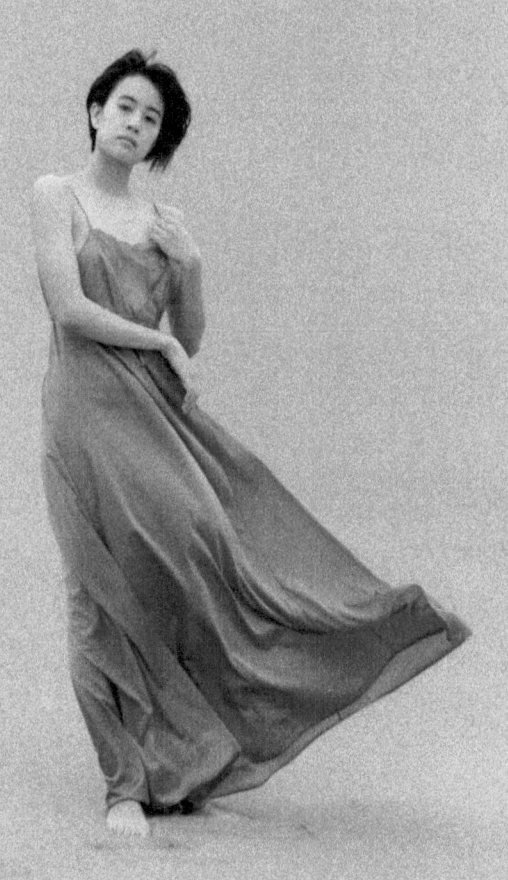

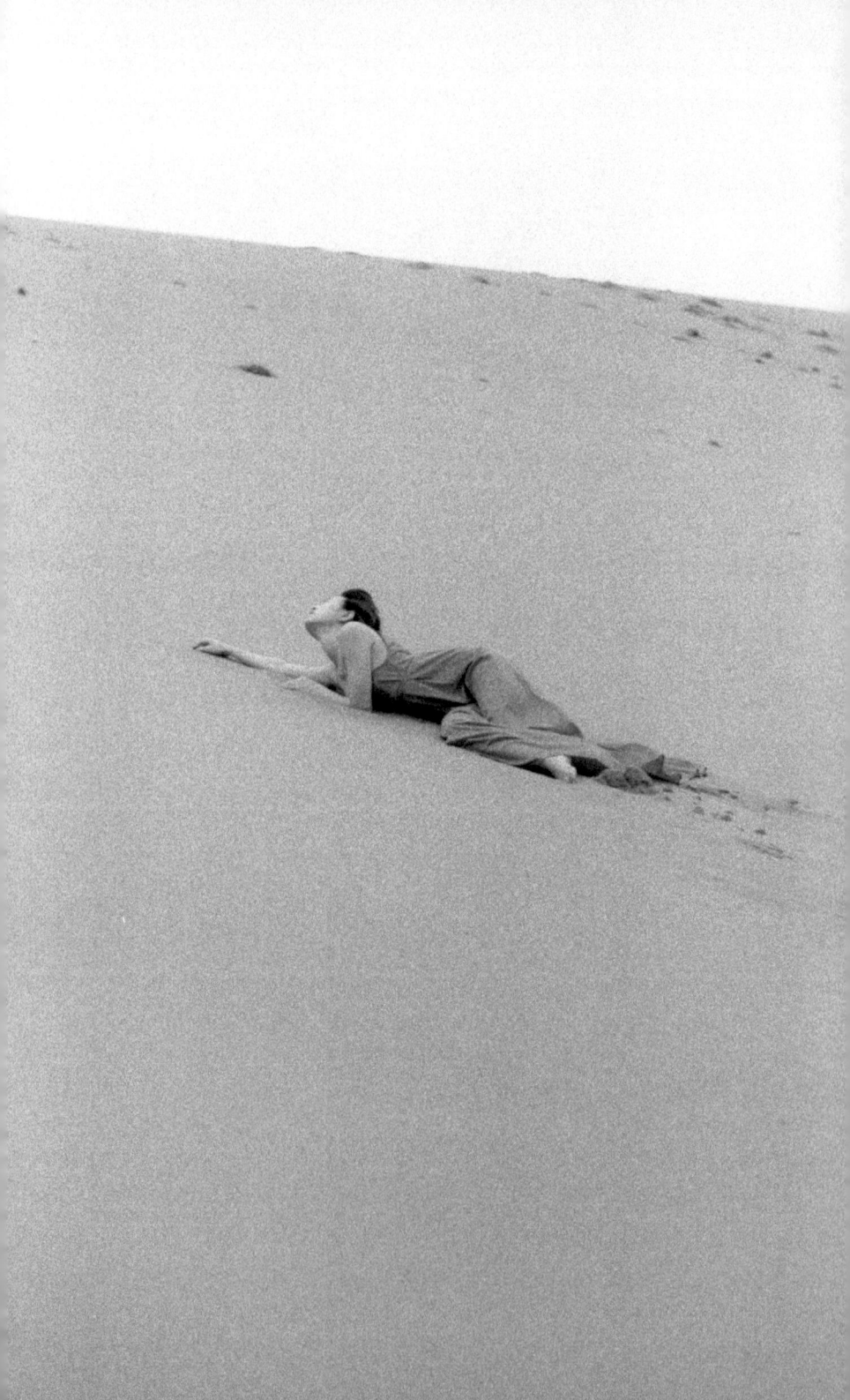

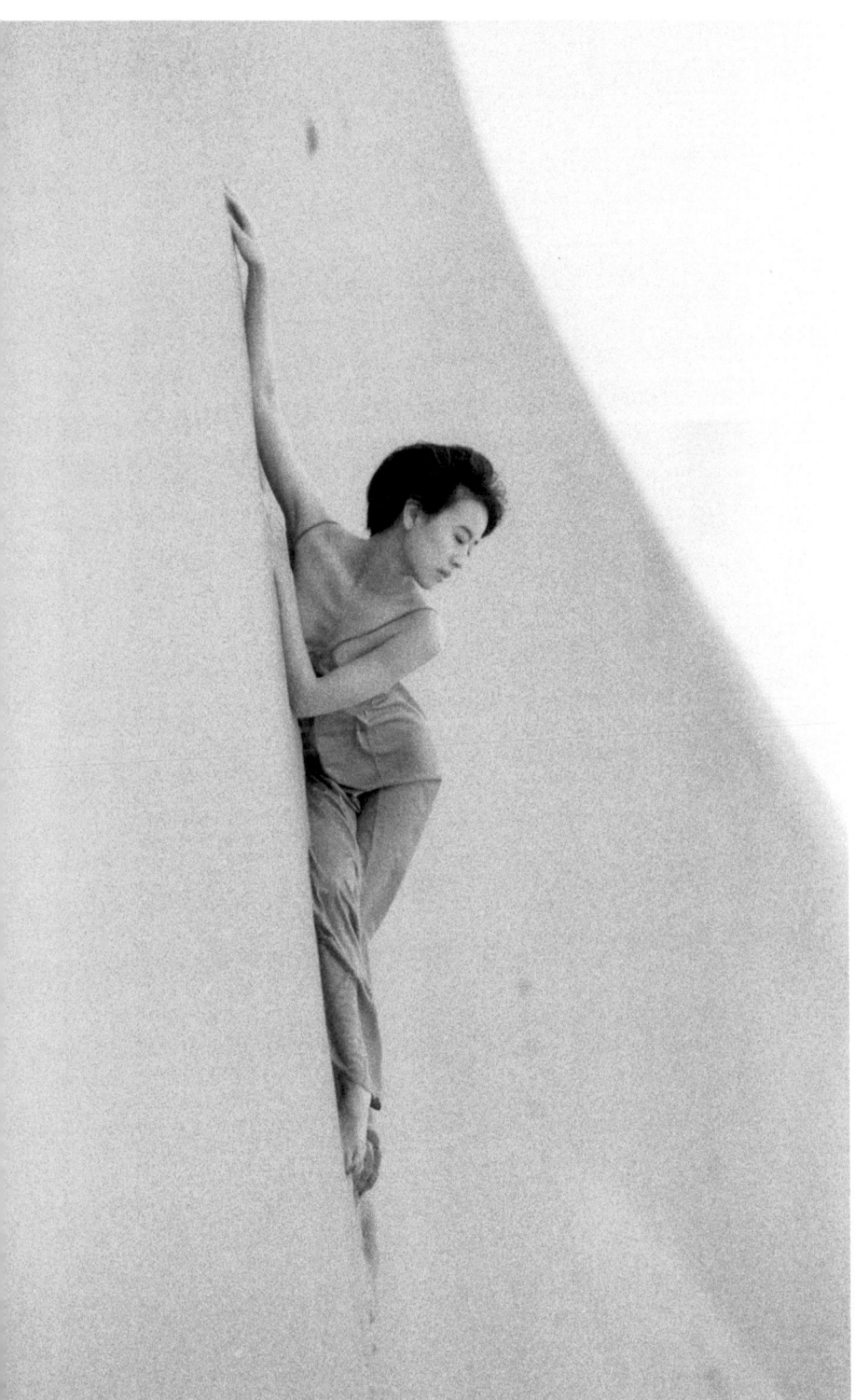

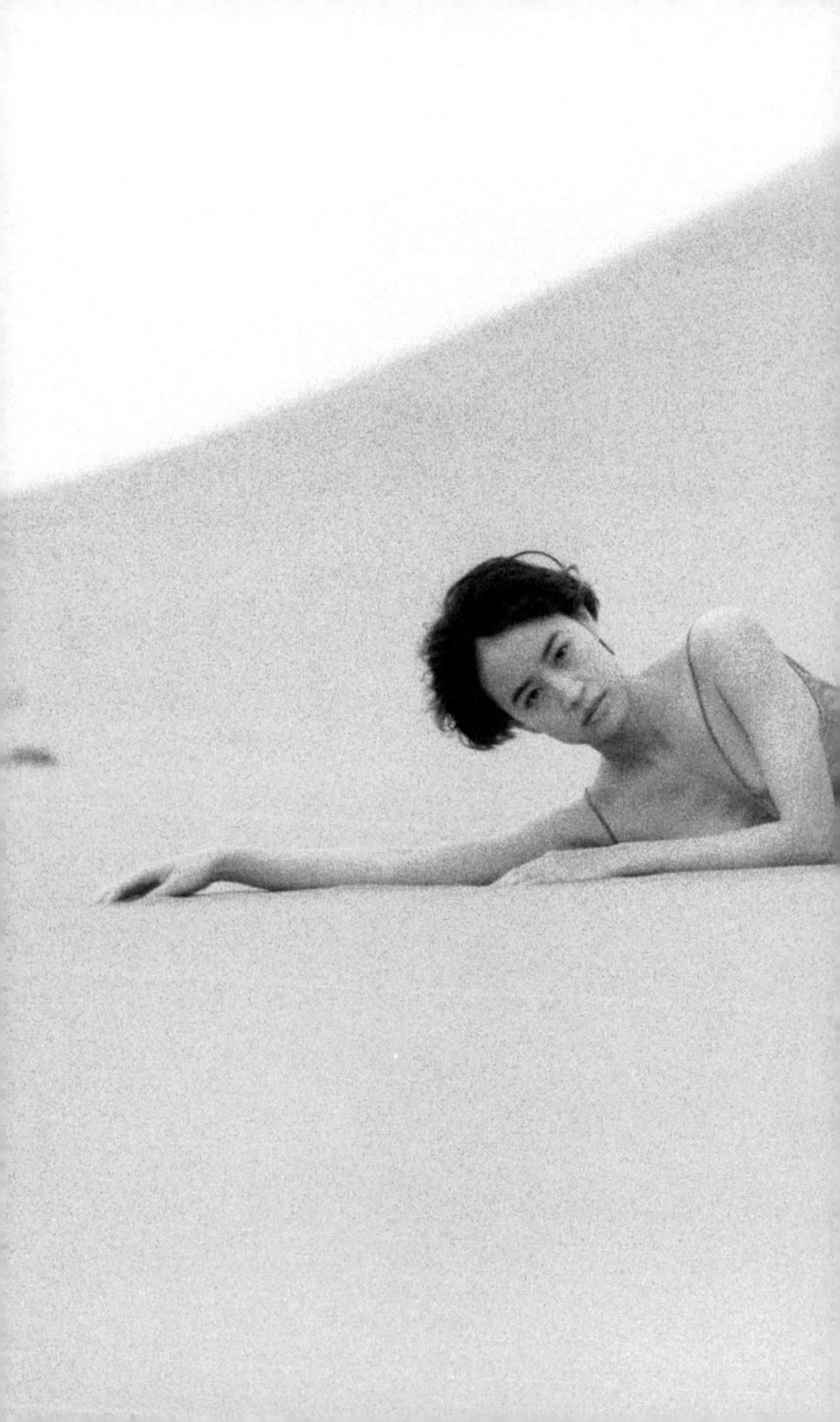

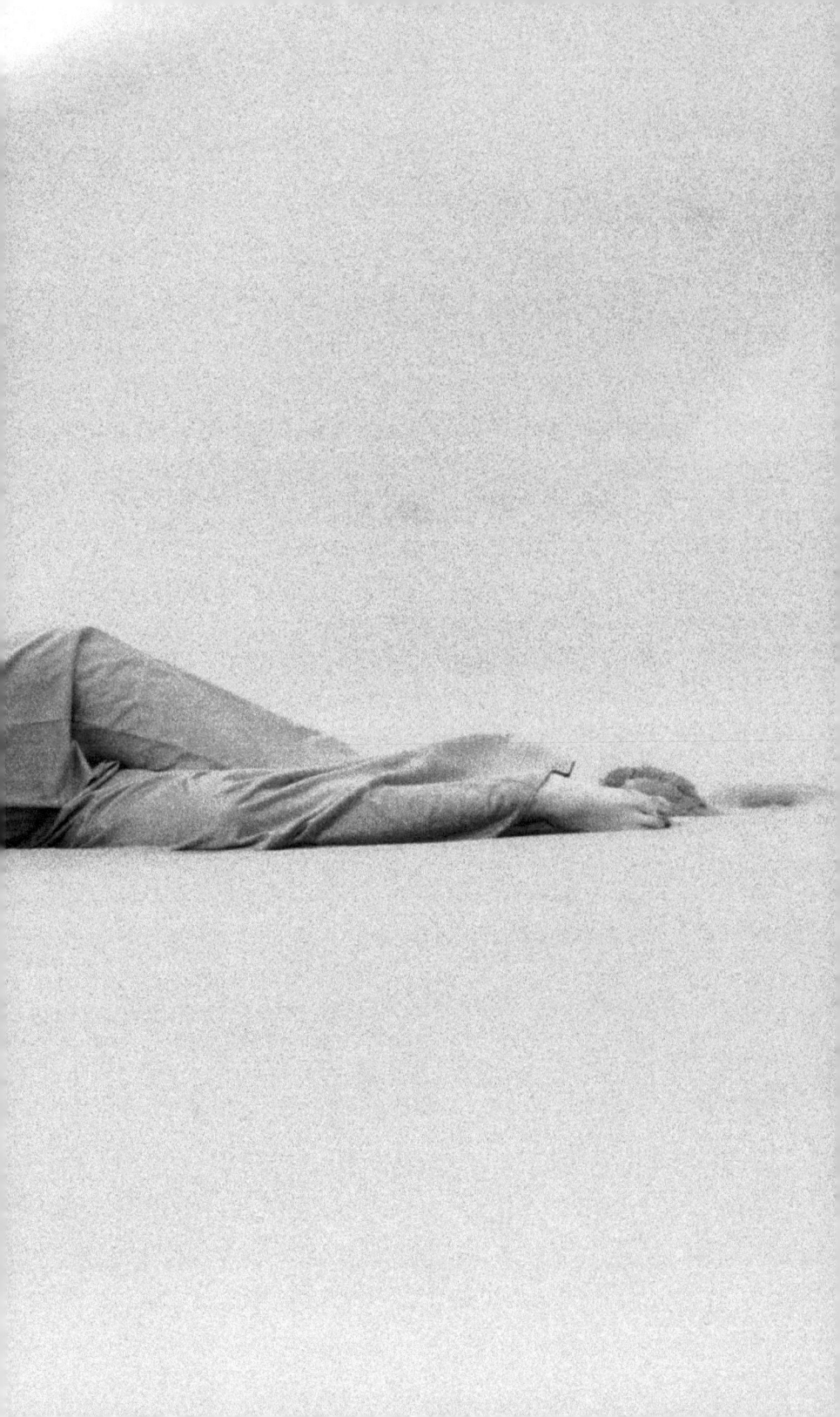

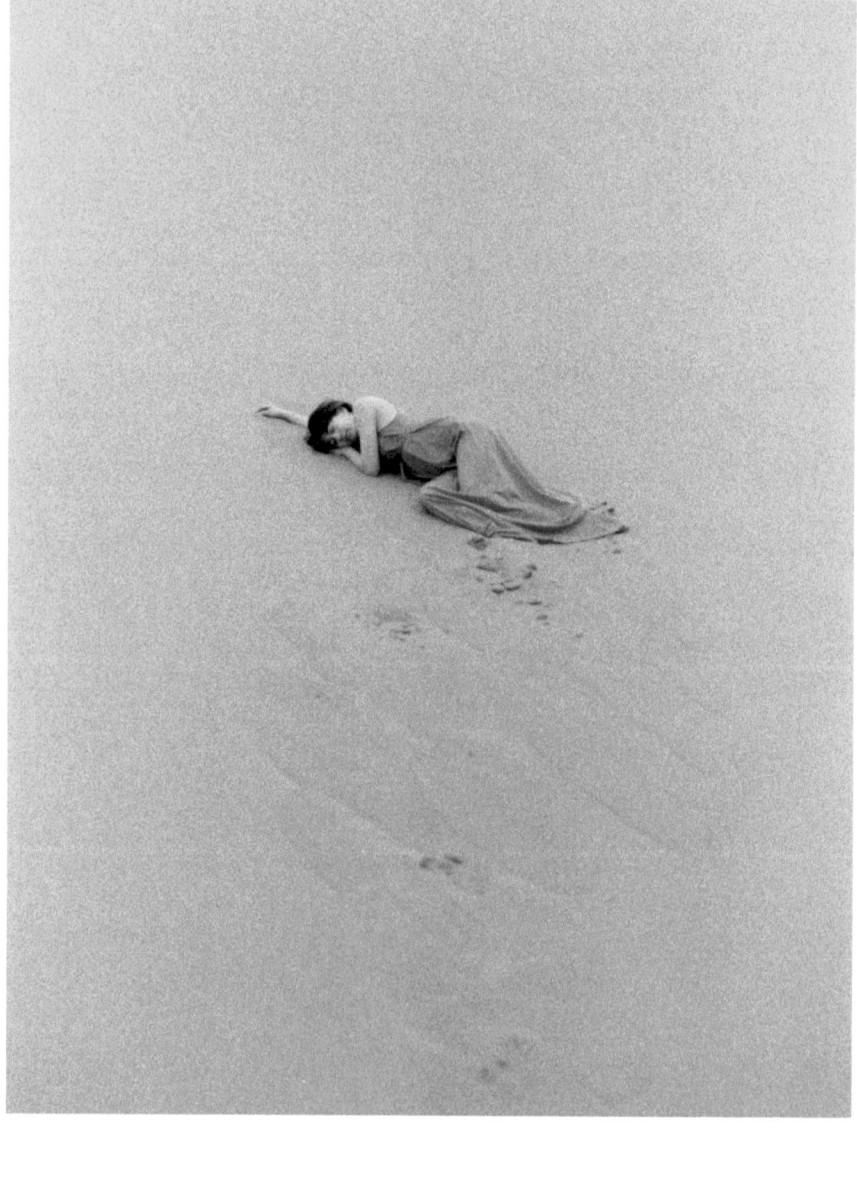

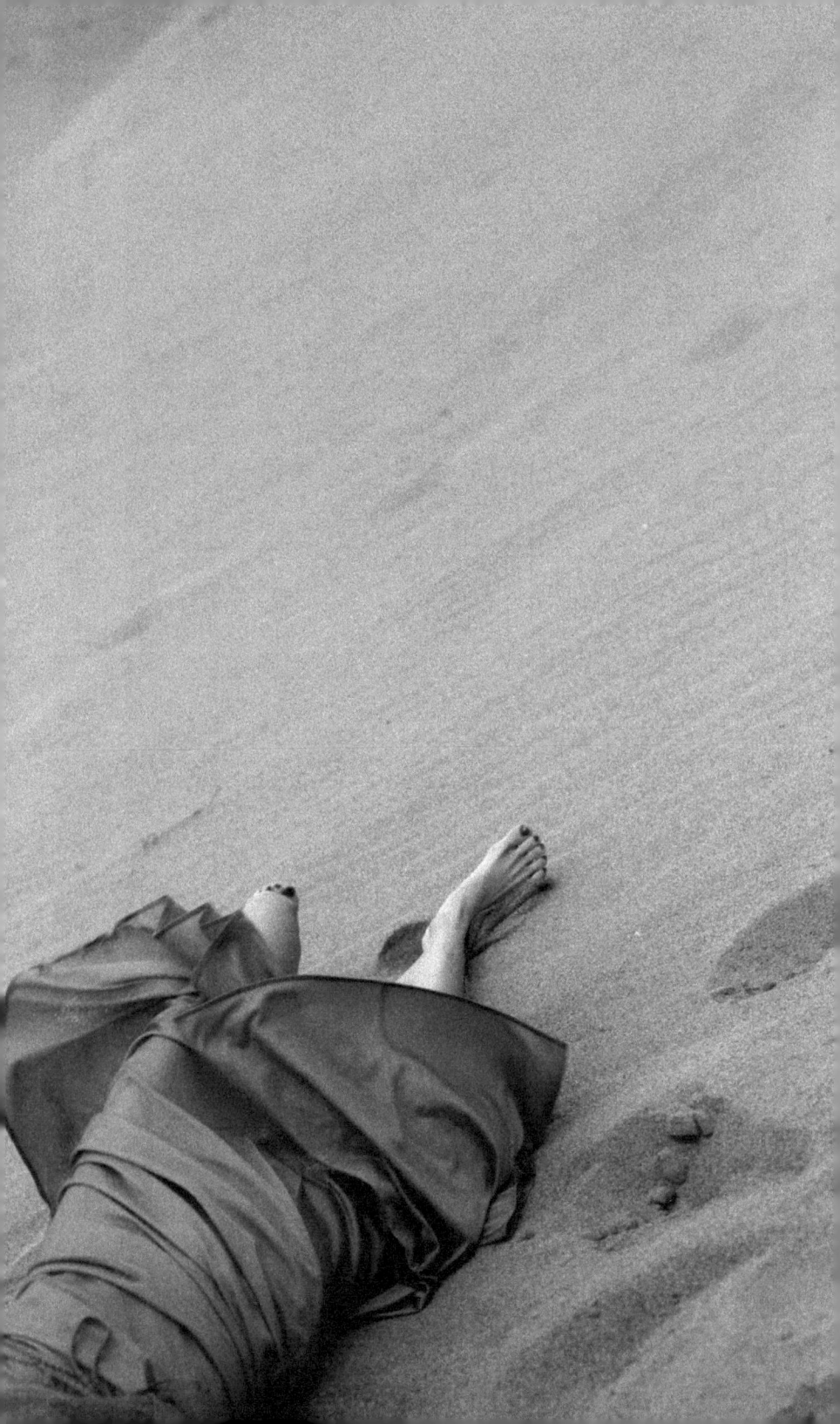

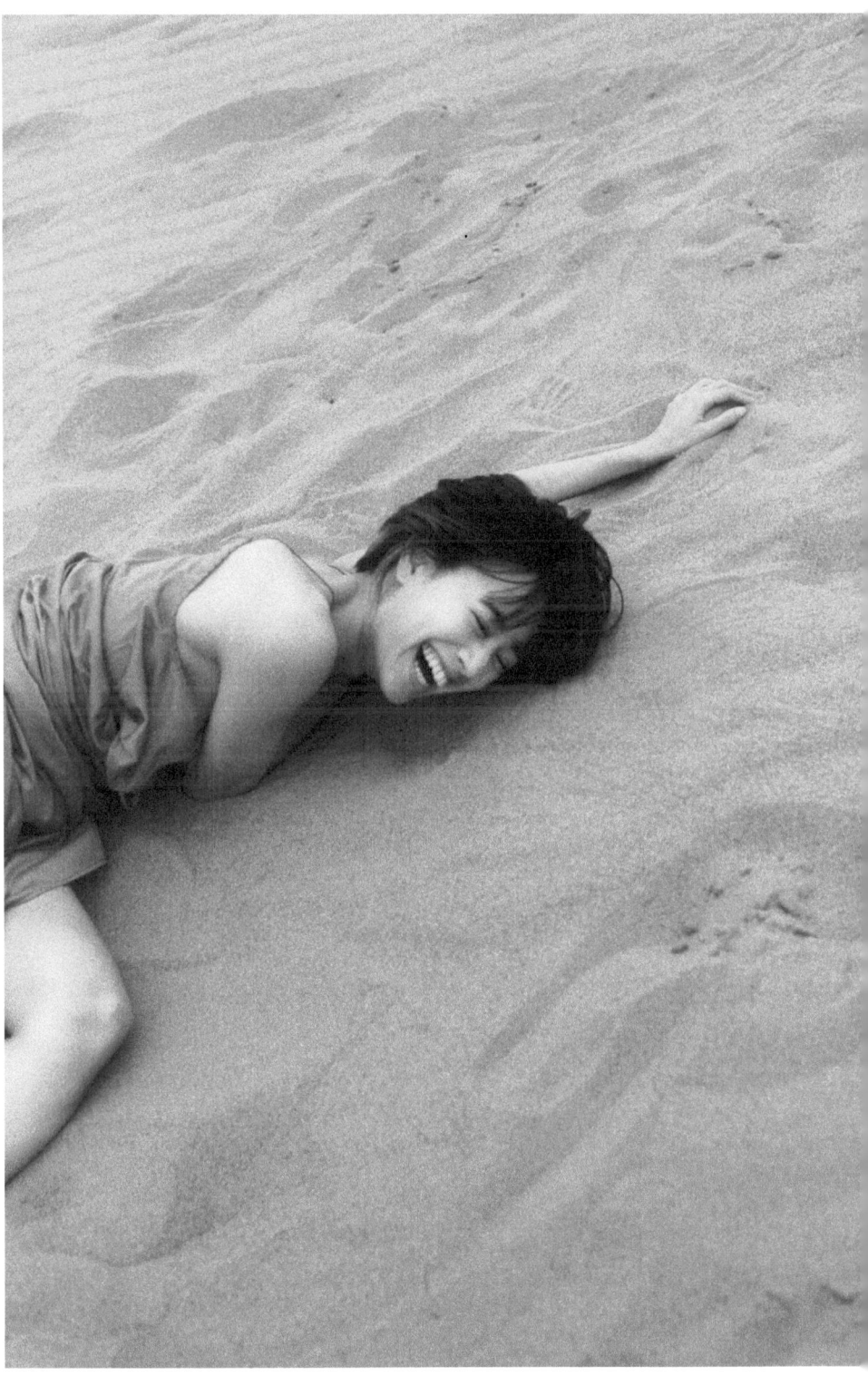

There is beauty in coming back to the emptiness of things···

Emptiness invites imagination for a dance.

It took me almost two years to finish the layout for this book. Took me even more to bring it to life. Like every seed infused with soul, it needed some time to grow and mature. I am glad I gave it time.

This print is imperfect, but there is something in imperfectness and simplicity that takes all the pretentiousness away. If I could, I would print every book myself, but for now - this is the best way to deliver my creation as widely as possible.

I left a few pages blank - for writing a poem or any thought that comes to your mind if you feel inspired.

I want to express my gratitude to Shizuka for being patient with delivering this project. Also, special thanks go to Sean, Mike, Sayaka, and every other person who helped me create and release it.

I hope you enjoy it.

Tim.

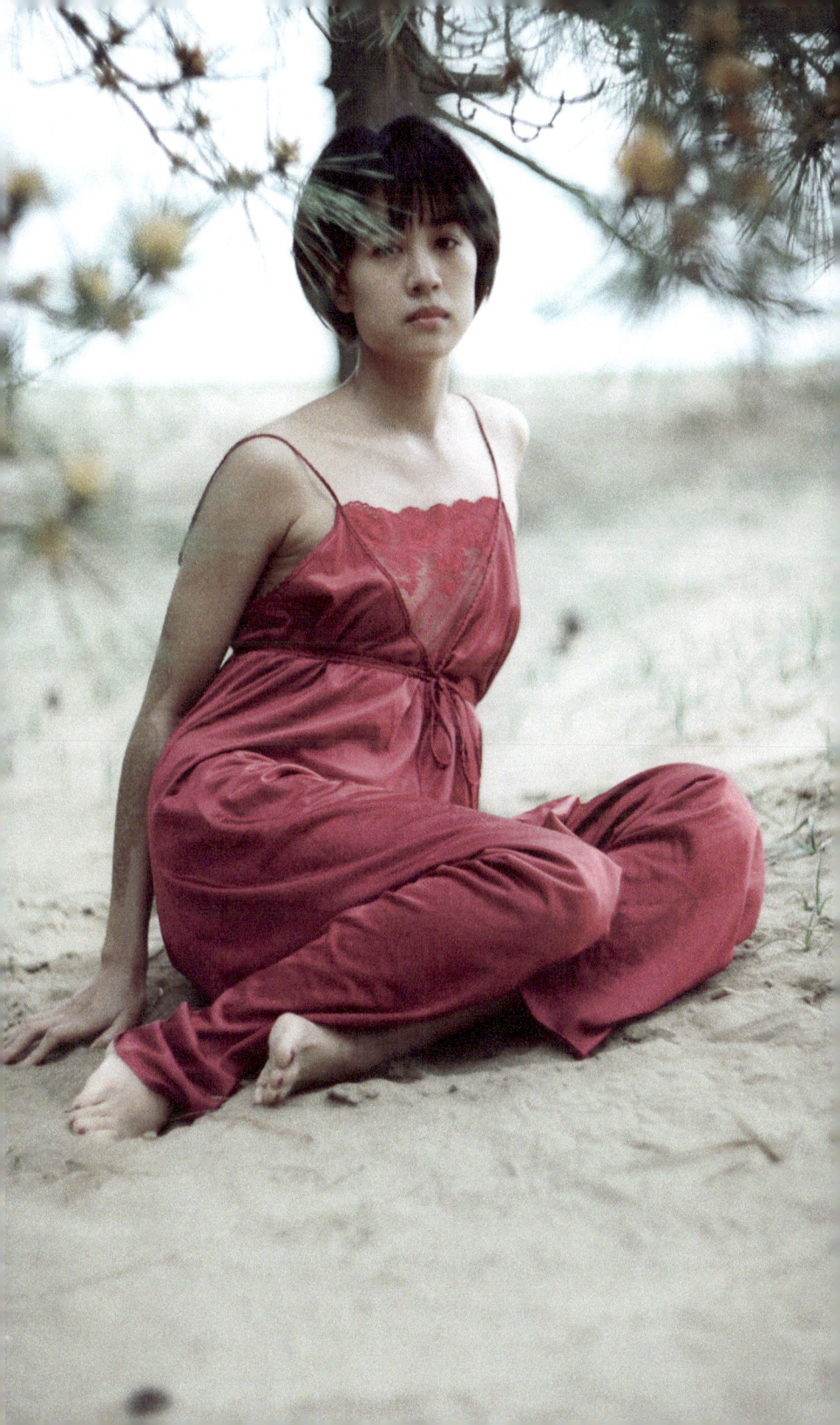

Woman in Dunes

performed by Shizuka Ishibashi
styling by Ryouhei Matsuda
photography and direction by Tim Gallo
All Rights Reserved.

www.ingramcontent.com/pod-product-compliance
Lightning Source LLC
Chambersburg PA
CBHW040319220526
45473CB00009B/2495